word for **TODAY**

Growing in Christ

1 Thessalonians: Steps to Christian maturity

PAUL MARSH

SCRIPTURE UNION
130 CITY ROAD, LONDON EC1V 2NJ

© Paul Marsh 1992

The right of Paul Marsh to be identified as author of
this work has been asserted by him in accordance with the
Copyright, Designs and Patents Act 1988.

First published 1992
by Scripture Union, 130 City Road, London EC1V 2NJ

ISBN 0 86201 764 5

British Library Cataloguing-in-Publication Data
A catalogue record for this book is available from the British Library.

Scripture quotations in this publication are from the Holy
Bible, New International Version, Copyright © 1973, 1987, 1984
International Bible Society. Published by Hodder and Stoughton

Designed by Mark Carpenter Design.

Phototypeset by Intype, London.
Printed and bound in Great Britain by Cox and Wyman Ltd, Reading.

CONTENTS

Thanks to:
Becky Totterdell and Campbell Grant, my editors, for whose hard work and encouragement I am grateful; Lyndy Rasmusen who tirelessly typed, retyped and kept on typing, even when she was tired!

Dedicated to:
My colleagues in Scripture Union, past and present, to whom I owe so much.

OTHER BOOKS IN THE SERIES

INTRODUCTION

More than anything else I wanted to grow. You see, I was short. Other boys in the class seemed to tower over me. Finally it happened, and inch by inch I gradually started catching up! It felt good to grow. As Christians, we have other compelling incentives for growth. We want to be like Christ, to live the life that the New Testament tells us about. And the good news is that we don't need to be stunted.

As we think together about growing in Christ we'll spend a fair amount of our time looking at Paul's first letter to the Thessalonians. It was a young church and Paul had only been able to spend a short time with them. Living in a pagan world, often surrounded by opposition, Paul knew how desperately they needed to grow. This letter shows clearly the major areas of growth that Paul knew were important for those young believers. They are areas of growth which are important for us, too.

The letter itself was written as a result of Timothy's

visit to Thessalonica. Paul and Silas had to take off quickly when opposition erupted, and it was important for the apostle to continue his outreach programme. Very soon Timothy was sent back to the city to carry on where Paul had left off. When Timothy finally caught up with Paul and Silas in Corinth and filled in the current picture for them, the apostle got down to writing this letter. Part of it is a review of his own visit. It also refers to the role he had given to Timothy, and the good news which Timothy had brought him.

All this means that in 1 Thessalonians Paul didn't set out to formulate a programme of Christian growth. Instead, he dealt with issues which were of immediate importance to the Thessalonians in view of what Timothy had been able to tell him. As it happens, his letter covers a range of important issues which are essential to our development as Christians. We'll not work progressively through Paul's letter, but draw out of it those aspects of his teaching and activity which were designed to help the Thessalonian Christians to grow as they followed Jesus day by day. We shall find our needs and experiences mirrored in theirs.

The chapter divisions in this book aren't intended to be a step-by-step guide to maturity. Faith, of course, is a good place to start, but the experience of love, commitment and holiness won't come to us 'packaged' in that order! These and other factors in growth will develop gradually and alongside each other – one of them stimulating the other. And the point at which opposition hits us will vary from person to person, though it's wise to remember that from the very birth of faith the Devil takes a close interest in us. On the other hand, there is the Holy Spirit who is always with us. So, although we look at his role and presence specifically in chapter 7, we'll discover along with the Thessalonians that he was with us right from the start and will live in us to the very end.

You'll notice as we look at the various aspects of growth that we fill out the teaching by drawing on other scriptures. Our main text will be the New International Version (NIV), although from time to time we'll also look at the Good News Bible (GNB) and the Revised Standard Version (RSV). For various reasons I have changed the names of some of the people mentioned in this book.

1
GROW IN
FAITH

At last Joan believed. It hadn't come easily, for when she arrived on the ski trip she thought she was a Christian already. Brought up to go to church, she rarely missed a Sunday. She read the Bible from time to time and sometimes prayed. She tried to do her best, to be kind and thoughtful, and to do what was right – at least, most of the time.

It was on the third evening of the ski trip that she came in after the evening session and said, 'I couldn't face coming to another Bible study this evening, so I went out onto the mountainside to think. I made a list. You can see it if you like.' And she handed it to me. It was quite brief: 'I go to church but it's boring. I try reading my Bible but it's usually as dry as dust. And when I pray, my prayers seem to bounce off the ceiling. I seem to be different from everyone here. I don't think I'm a real Christian, but I'd really like to be one.'

A day or two later Joan discovered a new and personal relationship with Jesus Christ when she asked him to forgive her sin and trusted him to be her Saviour.

On the final evening she shared her experience: 'When we first went up on the ski slopes there were the long icicles hanging from the hotel at Kleine Scheidegg, and they seemed to describe me as I compared myself with others on the trip. I felt spiritually cold and brittle. Today, down toward Grindelwald I saw a stream bursting out from underneath the snow where it started to thaw. It was bright in the sunlight, sparkling and alive. And that's just how I felt. I discovered that trusting Jesus to be my Saviour had turned my life around. I felt new and alive in a way that I'd never felt before.'

That's faith. Call it trust if you like; trusting Jesus to forgive your sins and make you into a new person.

FAITH MATTERS

Of course, it's possible to fool ourselves; to think like Joan that we're Christians, when in fact we're light years away from the reality. It's vitally important for each of us to be absolutely sure. That's why Paul sent Timothy back to Thessalonica while he and Silas concentrated on the opportunities for evangelism in Athens. He refers to this when he writes to them:

> 'But, brothers, when we were torn away from you for a short time (in person, not in thought), out of our intense longing we made every effort to see you. For we wanted to come to you – certainly I, Paul, did, again and again – but Satan stopped us . . . So when we could stand it no longer we thought it best to be left by ourselves in Athens. We sent Timothy, who is our brother and God's fellow-worker in spreading the gospel of Christ, to strengthen and encourage you in your faith, so that no-one would be unsettled by these trials. You know quite well that we were destined for them. In fact, when we were with you

we kept telling you that we would be persecuted. And
it turned out that way, as you well know. For this
reason, when I could stand it no longer, I sent to find
out about your faith. I was afraid that in some way
the tempter might have tempted you and our efforts
might have been useless.'

1 Thessalonians 2:17–3:5

Paul wanted to be sure that their faith was real. Normally
he would have spent a fair amount of time following up
his contacts, but on this occasion it wasn't possible. Luke
fills in the details in Acts 17:1–10 where he describes this
relatively brief period between Paul's arrival in Thessalonica and his sudden departure along with Silas.

'When they had passed through Amphipolis and
Apollonia, they came to Thessalonica, where there
was a Jewish synagogue. As his custom was, Paul went
into the synagogue, and on three Sabbath days he
reasoned with them from the Scriptures, explaining
and proving that the Christ had to suffer and rise
from the dead. "This Jesus I am proclaiming to you is
the Christ," he said. Some of the Jews were
persuaded and joined Paul and Silas, as did a large
number of God-fearing Greeks and not a few
prominent women.

But the Jews were jealous; so they rounded up
some bad characters from the market-place, formed
a mob and started a riot in the city. "They rushed to
Jason's house in search of Paul and Silas in order to
bring them out to the crowd. But when they did not
find them, they dragged Jason and some other
brothers before the city officials, shouting: "These
men who have caused trouble all over the world have
now come here, and Jason has welcomed them into

11

his house. They are all defying Caesar's decrees,
saying that there is another king, one called Jesus."
When they heard this, the crowd and the city officials
were thrown into turmoil. Then they put Jason and
the others on bail and let them go.

As soon as it was night, the brothers sent Paul
and Silas away to Berea.'

You get the picture – some believed, and many opposed.
The deteriorating situation made further work imposs-
ible and they were sent off in the middle of the night to
Berea.

It's obvious from 1 Thessalonians 2:17, 18 that Paul
knew those new Christians needed further help. He had
spent a minimum of time with them – just three weeks
in the synagogue – and we don't know how much longer
after they were thrown out by the Jews. Certainly, there
was no time to discover where everyone stood, nor had
there been an opportunity to establish and build them
up.

That's just where Timothy came in. Did you notice
his brief in 1 Thessalonians 3:2, 5? Look at verse 5 again:
'When I could stand it no longer, I sent to find out about
your faith.' That seems to have been Timothy's primary
task.

FIND OUT IF FAITH IS REAL

'To find out' translates a Greek word meaning, basically,
'to know'. That's how the Revised Standard Version
translates it. In fact, there are two Greek words to express
the idea 'to know'. One has the thought of knowing
with one's mind – being mentally convinced. The other

stresses a knowledge which comes from experience. It's the second of these that Paul uses here. Timothy had to find out from the experience of meeting these individuals just where they stood: seeing their lifestyle, discovering whether or not they were really changed, for that's what faith or trust in Christ achieves.

Faith changes us from the inside and it affects the way we live. Paul expressed it like this in 2 Corinthians 5:17: 'If anyone is in Christ, he is a new creation; the old has gone, the new has come!' That remains true. Faith which brings new birth is seen in the way we think, act and react, in how we respond to temptation; it affects our total lifestyle. So, being a Christian isn't just mentally accepting certain facts as true – facts about Jesus, who he is, and what he has done – it brings radical change. It is not merely my mind that's affected, important as this is, my emotions are involved, my will is motivated. I'm sorry for things I've done wrong and I repent. I'm grateful to Jesus for what he has done for me – dying on the cross for my sin. I trust him, too, not only to forgive my sins but to keep and help me day by day. I want to follow him, serve him, obey him, even though it's tough.

That was Timothy's task – to discover just where the Thessalonians stood. It's a check we can carry out on ourselves, asking; 'What do I believe? What does it mean to me? What effect is it having on my lifestyle?' These are questions which Joan had to ask, and in asking them she discovered a faith that was real. Of course, when we first become Christians we haven't got everything figured out. We don't understand all the implications of what we have believed. We can easily make mistakes in our desire to be obedient to what Jesus wants us to do.

This was well illustrated at the end of an evangelistic

outreach in a village just outside the city of Lahore in Pakistan where I used to work. A small section of the village, near the rubbish dump, was the home of the Christian community – nominally Christian. During a week of evangelism some responded, and at the close an older but senior member of the community came to us.

'I've trusted Jesus as my Saviour,' he said, 'and I have to put right quite a number of things in my life. The major problem is that I have two wives and I feel that isn't right. So I've decided to send off the old one and keep the younger woman.' What was his motivation? Was his profession of faith a convenient ploy, in order to get rid of some unwanted baggage?! Or did he really want to be obedient and have one wife – the right course of action as he saw it? It was gently pointed out to him that maybe it wasn't right to ditch either of the wives; that he had responsibilities to them both. Certainly there was no question of the older one being relegated to the scrap heap! It was important to 'find out about' his faith.

Probing, discerning, Timothy had to find out just where the Thessalonians stood, and he didn't have an easy task. Neither do we when we seriously question some of our motives in professing faith. It might be that we had an involvement with a Christian girlfriend or boyfriend, and that clouded the issue. So the question has to be answered; am I trusting Jesus to forgive and to save me, with no strings attached, no ulterior motives, no selfish objectives? It sometimes helps to clarify our thinking if we ask ourselves:

- Who is Jesus?
- What has he done for me?
- Why do I need him?

- What are my motives for becoming a Christian – *all* of them?
- What tends to hold me back from a complete commitment to Jesus?
- What changes will be seen in me when I truly follow Jesus?

Perhaps it's so far so good – we can respond honestly to the questions, confirming that our faith is real.

Real faith, however, needs to develop. That was Timothy's next task. Paul spells it out in chapter 3, verse 2: 'We sent Timothy . . . to strengthen and encourage you in your faith.' These are two words to get to grips with.

FAITH NEEDS STRENGTHENING

We discover first of all that faith needs to be strengthened. The Revised Standard Version translates it as 'to establish'. It gives the idea of being based on a firm foundation. Literally, the Greek word means 'to fix'. It implies that faith or trust is to be unshakeable. That's something to aim at. The force of the word comes out in Luke 9:51, 'Jesus resolutely set out for Jerusalem' (New International Version) '. . . he made up his mind and set out on his way to Jerusalem' (Good News Bible), '. . . he set his face to go up to Jerusalem' (Revised Standard Version). So, to put it literally, 'he fixed his face . . .' The various translations all add up to this; Jesus was unshakeable in his resolve to go up to Jerusalem, even though he knew full well that crucifixion and death awaited him there. It's that unshakeable characteristic of faith that God wants to see; a trust which when tested doesn't crumble. This is the thrust of chapter 3, verses 2, 3, 'We sent Timothy . . . to strengthen you in your faith, so that no-one would be unsettled by these trials.'

The Greek verb recurs several times in the New Testament, indicating the importance of being firmly established or strengthened as we grow in faith. Peter had a special role here. Anticipating his weakness and failure when Peter, scared to death in Caiaphas' court-yard, would deny even knowing him, Jesus said, 'Simon, Simon, Satan has asked to sift you as wheat. But I have prayed for you, Simon, that your faith may not fail. And when you have turned back, *strengthen* your brothers' (Luke 22:31, 32). Peter would know from his own experience of failure how vital it was to be strong and immovable. That experience would help him as he tried in subsequent years to strengthen others.

It is good to know that in addition to the help a Timothy or a Peter can give, God has his own ways, too, of strengthening Christians. He himself works directly in our lives. In tough situations, in temptation or per-secution, he is there to strengthen and make us increasingly unshakeable. Take a look at 2 Thessalonians 3:3: '. . . The Lord is faithful, and he will strengthen and protect you from the evil one.' And 1 Peter 5:10, '. . . The God of all grace, who called you to his eternal glory in Christ, after you have suffered a little while, will restore you and make you strong, firm and steadfast.' So God has his own ways of building his strength into our characters.

There is a sense, of course, in which we personally have a major responsibility for strengthening ourselves in our faith. Getting God's word into our hearts and minds is an important element. Weak Christians are often those who don't know their Bibles. And the converse is true; those who are strong have taken God's strengthening word into their minds and hearts.

This was made strikingly clear some years ago when I was visiting Singapore. It was just prior to the fall of Saigon in South Vietnam. Among the hundreds of Westerners being flown out of Saigon was a friend who landed in Singapore. He recorded his final contact with an eighteen-year-old South Vietnamese girl who met him at the airport just before he left.

'I know there's no hope of my escaping the Communists who are about to capture the city,' she told him. 'And I'm not at all sure just what will happen to me when they take over. Perhaps they'll take away my Bible. In case they do, I've started to memorise it, and I'm beginning with Peter's first letter.'

Why Peter's first letter? I was left in no doubt when back in my room I read through the letter once more and came to such verses as: 'For it is commendable if a man bears up under the pain of unjust suffering because he is conscious of God. But how is it to your credit if you receive a beating for doing wrong and endure it? But if you suffer for doing good and you endure it, this is commendable before God. To this you were called, because Christ suffered for you, leaving you an example, that you should follow in his steps . . . If you are insulted because of the name of Christ, you are blessed, for the Spirit of glory and of God rests on you. If you suffer, it should not be as a murderer or thief or any other kind of criminal, or even as a meddler. However, if you suffer as a Christian, do not be ashamed, but praise God that you bear that name' (1 Peter 2:19–21; 4:14–16). Her faith was strong – strengthened by God's word.

We can work at it, too:

- Scripture Union notes can really help to establish our faith as we study God's word day by day.
- Memorise scripture. Then the Holy Spirit can bring it to our minds just when it's needed.
- Regular involvement in the life of a living, local church is important – sharing in house-group activities and Bible study.
- Forming strong Christian friendships will be a positive help.

And *we're* responsible for all of these.

FAITH NEEDS ENCOURAGEMENT

Timothy had a third responsibility. We discover quickly that faith needs to be encouraged as we follow Jesus. So Paul writes: 'We sent Timothy . . . to encourage you in your faith' (1 Thessalonians 3:2). Our trust in Jesus grows with encouragement. This word encouragement implies help. That's how the Good News Bible translates it: 'We sent him . . . to help your faith.' The Greek word has within it the idea of 'called alongside to help'. That's the meaning of Paraclete – one of the names of the Holy Spirit – and it describes well one of the roles that he has in our lives.

The year 1983 found me in the mountains of Baltistan, Pakistan. Driving in a jeep along the Karakoram highway we hugged the rugged mountainside, with the River Indus hundreds of feet below. It was early spring. Tiny, terraced fields above the far bank of the Indus were being prepared for sowing. Clinging tenaciously to the mountainside, one narrow field was about to be ploughed. At one end of the field stood a single yoked ox, with two men at the plough, and I wondered where the second ox could be. Then in total amazement I saw the second man stoop under the yoke. Side by side he and the ox went the short length of the terraced field, pulling the hand-steered plough. At the end of the field, holding his side of the yoke, he coaxed the ox around. Then I realised that at this far point of the terrace the field was too narrow for two oxen to turn. Below, the mountainside fell sharply away, but the ox turned safely, helped by the farmer who shared the yoke. Together they went on, tackling turn after turn until the field was ploughed.

Jesus said, 'Take my yoke upon you and learn from me' (Matthew 11:29). He promises to stick close to us and to help us as we learn from him — at all times and in all situations. So the Thessalonians needed Jesus and Timothy alongside them.

Our faith is built up by people who get alongside us, so it's important to have Christian friends. We need lots of help, especially in the early days of our faith, but it's an ongoing need. Timothy was to help in that kind of way — safeguarding, guiding, 'so that no-one would be unsettled by these trials'. We can't do without helpful, experienced Christians who can advise, caution and teach. That's how faith is encouraged, and how new Christian helpers, encouragers, are made. Faith grows as a result.

Check up on your faith; if it's help or encouragement you need, try to form a friendship and relationship that will build up your faith. Find a church or house group that meets that need. Or has God got for you a Timothy role?

Certainly, Timothy and the Thessalonian Christians didn't disappoint Paul. When Timothy finally caught up with the apostle in Corinth, he had great news to share, the Thessalonian Christians' faith was in good working order! To use Paul's words: 'Timothy has just now come to us from you and has brought good news about your faith and love' (3:6). Significantly, it's a faith which from that moment colours Paul's prayers: 'We continually remember before our God and Father your work produced by faith' (1:3).

PUT YOUR FAITH INTO PRACTICE

Notice how Paul refers to 'your work produced by faith'. As we have seen, faith is not merely the acceptance of Bible facts. Faith works in our lives, affects situations, transforms events. The Good News Bible emphasises this: '. . . you put your faith into practice.'

We get the first inkling of this in Acts 17:10: 'As soon as it was night, the brothers sent Paul and Silas away to Berea.' Imagine the situation. A hostile mob has caused a riot in the city and they are after Paul and Silas' blood. Jason has been arrested and dragged through the streets. Finally, he's released on bail, but the charge of 'defying Caesar's decrees' is still to be answered. Not only Paul and Silas, but the entire newly-founded Christian group are under threat. It could mean death. Now read again verse 10; 'As soon as it was night, the brothers sent Paul and Silas away to Berea.' The Thessalonians might well have said to Paul and Silas, 'We're grateful that you came. We believe in Jesus and it's wonderful! But, Paul, if we ever needed you, it's right now. You know how to sort out the authorities – after all, you're a Roman citizen. You can handle this one.' But it wasn't like that. Imagine the conversation, 'Paul, thanks for coming. You said it would be tough. So it is, but God's with us. With his help, we'll handle the Jews and the authorities. But whatever happens, you're best out of here. Tonight some of the brothers will take you to Berea.'

That was faith put into practice. That kind of faith could go on growing. One act of witness, trembling but still trusting God to help, leads to further acts, with a faith strengthened by the experience of God's help already given. Of course, there will be opposition, as we'll discover in the next chapter, but it can be faced with faith that grows, as God is proved to be reliable. This growing faith depends, not on theological degrees, tolerant societies or favourable cultures; but on a living God. And, amazingly, it thrives in adverse conditions.

Jivan was born into a nominal Christian community in Pakistan. He grew up illiterate; a coolie working in the fields. He became a Christian and joined the growing church established in his own village. But what about the surrounding villages of the Punjab? They, too, needed to hear about Christ, to be taught and strengthened to live for him. A four-day annual convention, he thought, might help; four days of teaching to build up faith. But then Jivan's own faith was challenged. How could he feed and sleep 100 or 200 Christians from the surrounding villages? Day after day his prayer of faith grew in expectancy: 'Lord we need sacks of wheat flour. We need rice. We need vegetables. Lord, we need meat!' And as the convention day dawned, a joyous, illiterate, believing coolie saw wheat, rice, flour, vegetables in abundance. And not only that, live chickens were brought squawking to the front of the meeting as a contribution for lunch! There was even a goat on the hoof!

Jivan's experience isn't merely an interesting story.

It's an example, and an encouragement to put our own faith into positive action. There is no doubt about it, faith grows. Give it the right conditions, put it into practice day by day, and there will be results.

• How might God want you to use your faith – in relation to people, personal needs, the outreach and growth of your local church?
• Think through and identify areas in your own life where your trust or faith needs strengthening. Areas, perhaps, where you've failed. Figure out steps you can take for your faith to grow.
• What part do leisure activities play in holding you back or helping you forward? What about the books you read; the programmes you watch and the places you visit?
• What help or encouragement to a growing faith do you find in your local church? Is there a lack of which you are conscious? Talk it over with one of your leaders.
• Whose faith can you encourage in your local fellowship? What are their needs?
• Look at your work situation. Who needs to trust Jesus as their Saviour? How can you help? Are there other Christians? How could you be of encouragement to them?
• Remember your family. Was that where you came to know Jesus, or do they still need to trust him as their Saviour? What do they see of your faith? What are their particular needs as Christians or non-Christians? What would you like Jesus to do for them?

As we tackle these issues, we'll discover that Jesus comes alongside to help, yoking himself to us, teaching and encouraging us. Of course there'll be set-backs, for the Devil is a real enemy, but faith that's tested is faith that grows.

2

GROW THROUGH OPPOSITION

It wasn't easy for Shah Mohammed Shah. Kneeling on the cold concrete floor in a little room in Mumtazabad on the outskirts of Multan in Pakistan, Shah listened as his friend asked, 'Shah, do you believe that Jesus Christ is the Son of God?'

'Yes, I do,' was Shah's response in a soft, measured, but certain voice.

'Do you believe, Shah, that the Lord Jesus Christ died on the cross for your sins?'

'Yes, I do,' came the same convinced reply.

Together they prayed, Shah confirming his trust in the Lord Jesus and committing himself to him for the future, whatever that would hold. Now we watched Shah as he cycled off down the road toward his home by the canal which flowed outside the city. The evening air was cold.

Once inside the house, Shah told his family the step he had taken. There were his parents, his wife and their little baby. The response was immediate. That night they separated out his dishes. No more shared food. No more access to the pump in the courtyard. But worse, far worse, they took away his wife and baby. He no longer had a home or a family. Next morning when he arrived at the electrical shop where he worked for his uncle, he discovered that he no longer had a job. The news of his decision to follow Christ had gone ahead of him.

OPPOSITION CAN BE TOUGH

Opposition can be tough, even violent. Perhaps Shah was fortunate to escape with his life that night. Opposition for most of us is less stark and terrifying, though Shah's experience is still a common occurrence in many parts of the world. To declare faith in Jesus Christ, to commit one's life to him, was in Paul's day an equally dangerous step to take. Jesus had said so quite plainly: 'If anyone would come after me, he must deny himself and take up his cross and follow me' (Mark 8:34). A cross had one meaning only. Wherever one lived: in the Jewish, Greek or Roman world, the reaction was likely to be the same. The Jewish authorities had hated Jesus and killed him. They had hated Paul, too. Now writing to the Thessalonians he reminds them of this common experience which had become theirs:

> 'You suffered from your own countrymen the same
> things those churches suffered from the Jews, who
> killed the Lord Jesus and the prophets and also drove
> us out.'   *1 Thessalonians 2:14, 15*

Paul knew about opposition. In Ephesus Demetrius set the whole city against him (Acts 19: 23–41). In Philippi the authorities had him and Silas publicly stripped, flogged and thrown into prison (Acts 16:16–40). No doubt when he arrived in Thessalonica (Acts 17) his back was still bruised and sore from the beating he had received. Some months later, writing to the Thessalonians from Corinth, he recalls his experience – and his reaction:

> 'We had previously suffered and been insulted in Philippi, as you know, but with the help of our God we dared to tell you his gospel in spite of strong opposition.'
> *1 Thessalonians 2:2*

Paul made sure that the Christians in Thessalonica knew what to expect. And in his letter he underlines what he had already made clear:

> '. . . when we were with you, we kept telling you that we would be persecuted. And it turned out that way, as you well know.'
> *1 Thessalonians 3:4*

CHRISTIANS ARE A THREAT

Does it all sound unreal in a western context and in a society which claims to be tolerant; happy for everyone to 'do their own thing'? It's quite possible that as you try to be loyal to Jesus where you live or work, you may not seem to provoke a flicker of opposition. There's disinterest, perhaps, even appreciation. That can go on for weeks, months, even longer. But in most cases, sooner or later, an action, word or attitude will light the fuse.

Go through this check-list and rate how often you could be marked out as 'different' in your workplace.

- Fiddling accounts or personal expenses
- Misuse of office facilities or equipment

- Bad language – swearing, blasphemy
- Dirty stories
- Involvement in some kinds of office parties
- Lying to solve a problem
- Gossip
- Time wasting and clock-watching
- Absenteeism

You can add to the list.

And there will be a reaction. It could be that you are:

- marginalised
- avoided or ignored
- picked on
- denied promotion
- appreciated for your integrity – and promoted
- valued for your contributions
- asked to explain what makes you tick.

There's the total mix of experience which makes up our lives. How do you handle it?

But the fact remains, wherever they are and in whatever century they are born, Christians are again and again regarded as a threat. Their lives are a rebuke to injustice and corruption. Both Jesus and Paul make the issue clear: 'If they persecuted me, they will persecute you also,' said Jesus (John 15:20). Paul reminds Timothy, 'Everyone who wants to live a godly life in Christ Jesus will be persecuted' (2 Timothy 3:12). So, if in fact we are persecuted, that puts us in the same company as Jesus and Paul – good company!

In this way we discover that hostility, when it comes, usually surfaces at a practical level. It may be, for example, when we refuse to compromise.

Susan worked in a warehouse in Glasgow for a company dealing mainly in imports. Goods broken in transit were charged against insurance. From time to time, however, when articles were being unpacked something would be dropped and broken. The common reaction was, 'Charge it up to insurance – broken in transit.' Susan's problem when she dropped something was just this: 'It wasn't broken in transit. I dropped it, and the responsibility's mine.' Her reaction cut across accepted practices. She was the odd one out. Her sense of integrity offended those around her. Finally, they reacted so strongly that Susan had to leave. That was the price of living 'a godly life', as Paul called it.

We quickly discover with Paul and the Thessalonians that the Christian life lived uncompromisingly provokes a reaction. And if we never experience any kind of opposition, it might be worthwhile asking why.

SATAN KNOWS HOW TO ATTACK

The Devil is someone to be reckoned with. Where there's opposition, he's around. He may act directly or indirectly, but he'll be there. Jesus experienced his direct attack in the desert (Matthew 4:1–11), and those assaults continued right up to the crucifixion. Sometimes Satan comes to us indirectly, cunningly using people. There was Peter, with the best of intentions, trying to dissuade Jesus from going to the cross. 'Out of my sight, Satan!' was Jesus' response to an astonished Peter (Mark 8:31–33). Jesus knew the Devil's ways. Paul also knew that just as Satan had tried to destroy Jesus, so, directly or indirectly he would attack the

Thessalonians. That was his main worry when he sent Timothy to them:

> 'I was afraid that in some way the tempter might have tempted you and our efforts might have been useless.'   1 Thessalonians 3:5

SEE HOW THE DEVIL OPERATES

Let's think about the Devil for a moment and see how he operates. Knowing the enemy helps us to stand up to him. His names and descriptions spell out his character.

Tempter

As we've just seen, Paul calls him the 'tempter' in 1 Thessalonians 3:5. The meaning's plain: he tempts us to do what is wrong. It began with Adam and Eve (Genesis 3), Jesus experienced it (Matthew 4:1–11), and we're not exempt.

Satan

Paul also called him 'Satan'. The word means adversary, opponent, enemy. And he's a powerful enemy at that. Look at 1 Thessalonians 2:18 where Paul writes:

> 'We wanted to come to you – certainly I, Paul, did, again and again – but Satan stopped us.'

We don't know how he did it, but he succeeded. Possibly, it was the ongoing opposition which he had stirred up in Thessalonica, making it a 'no go area' so far as Paul was concerned. Certainly, he knew that Paul was anxious to develop strong believers who were firm in their faith. And Satan is opposed to strong Christians; he wants to keep them weak.

Evil one
Then Paul refers to him as 'the evil one' in 2 Thessalonians 3:3. His personality and plans are all evil.

God of this age
In 2 Corinthians 4:4 the apostle describes him as 'the god of this age', and here Paul refers to his ability to blind the minds of unbelievers. So he continues to blind people to the truth, to the reality of God's love and his tremendous plans for them. It's 'the god of this age' who's adept at manipulating the media, at stimulating selfishness, greed, lust, and immorality. Analyse the mass media advertising; what does it appeal to in us?

Enemy – roaring lion
Peter never forgot Satan's subtlety and power to manipulate. Perhaps it was with the memory of his own failure in seeking to dissuade Jesus from going to the cross, that he wrote years later: 'Your enemy the Devil prowls around like a roaring lion looking for someone to devour' (1 Peter 5:8). He had made mincemeat of Peter, not only in persuading him that Jesus mustn't throw his life away (Mark 8:32), but also in Caiaphas' courtyard, where he experienced the Devil's ability to make him so scared that he denied even knowing Jesus (Mark 14:66–72).

Let's look back to Shah for a moment. Satan knew how to work on him. He was determined to break Shah down. And he did, although it took two full years. As an electrician, Shah tried to get work. The word went round the city that Shah was a Christian. Every application was refused. For a short period he went to Lahore to get a full electrician's qualification. Then once more he returned to Multan. He had now changed his name from Shah Mohammed Shah to Shah Masih, marking himself out clearly as a Christian. Again, constant rejections accompanied every attempt he made to obtain work.

Finally, at the end of two years Shah called at a factory office where an electrician was needed. His qualifications were right – but they had been for nearly two years now. Would it be another refusal?

'What's your name?' the man behind the desk asked him.

'Shah Mohammed Shah.' he responded. And he got the job. He was no longer Shah Masih. He had hidden his faith.

From that point the scene changed. Shah Mohammed Shah got back his wife and his child. He was welcomed into his parents' home. But he had lost the joy of following Christ faithfully. He no longer met with Christians to worship. He had no witness. More children were born but there was an ache in Shah's heart. He kept in contact with his friend who originally had brought him to Christ, and with a few other believers. But Shah was sad – sad for some ten years – until one day with a broken heart he came back and had the joy again of following the Lord Jesus.

SATAN IS DEFEATED

Satan needn't have the last word! He didn't with Shah. Peter discovered that, and, while recognising him as a roaring lion, he went on to write: 'Resist him, standing firm in the faith' (1 Peter 5:9). It's clear then why Paul was so anxious to ensure that the Thessalonian Christians became firm or strong in their faith, that, to use his words, 'no-one would be unsettled by these trials' (1 Thessalonians 3:3).

Satan isn't an all-powerful enemy. Christ defeated him, and all those who follow Jesus can defeat him, too. Paul knew this, and although for some reason the Devil prevented him from getting back to strengthen the Thessalonians, Timothy was able to go instead. There is always a way to conquer Satan.

Even so, Satan is ready to pounce whenever he gets the opportunity! Watch out for him. One element that sometimes throws us is his speed of attack. They soon discovered this in Thessalonica. Acts 17:2, 5–9 tells us that after just three weeks of teaching in the synagogue, the Jewish community went into action. We're not guaranteed a six-month honeymoon period when we come to Jesus – sometimes not even six days or hours!

Remember the speed of attack that Shah experienced: on the night of his conversion they took away his wife and his child; the next morning his job. The opposition we experience probably won't be so sudden or extreme, but it will come and, probably, quickly. Maybe your changed life, or a few words spoken about Jesus will spark things off and give Satan a chance to react. Or maybe, like me, you let fear get the better of you – early on or at the start of a new situation. And suddenly Satan has a field day.

It was my first night in the RAF. Five of us found ourselves in a room together. Everything was new, exciting – all five eager to fly! A bit daunting, too. As we sorted out our blankets and made up our beds, a

31

fellow eighteen-year-old beside me pulled out a Bible and started to read. He made his mark. There'd be opposition, but he'd face it. My Bible was there – in my bag out of sight, and there it stayed. For some stupid reason I was too scared to get it out. The Devil knew how to shut me up, and that sudden attack led on to three years of silence.

God is still looking for Pauls and Timothys to get alongside us to warn, prepare, to strengthen and encourage, so that we won't be unsettled by these trials. And to remind us that persecution will come (1 Thessalonians 3:3, 4).

OPPOSITION TAKES VARIOUS FORMS

It's not long before we realise that opposition takes a variety of forms. We may discover with Susan that it's at work where the trouble starts. For Shah, on the other hand, opposition began with the family – work problems didn't surface until the next morning!

Whenever or wherever the attack, it's important to remember that the real attacker is Satan. People are his tools – people we may love and respect – they can be parents, brothers or sisters, long-standing friends, colleagues or neighbours. So, when the pressure is on, it's often a help to remind ourselves that it's not so much them, as the Devil who's getting at us.

Josephine's initial opposition started at home. She came to Christ through a Billy Graham broadcast – and she was absolutely alone. From the outset Dad was the problem. He just couldn't stomach the idea of 'Christianity'; the gospel certainly wasn't good news so far as he was concerned. And Josephine went into the office on one occasion with a black eye as evidence of the fact. Her two sisters turned to Christ; her mum years later responded, but Dad seemed adamant. Josephine's Bible was anathema, and if she wanted to read or pray, the loo down the garden was the only possibility. Opposition came quickly and it lasted for years. But consistent living – three changed daughters living in the house – and plain courage from the Holy Spirit, saw a mellowing. So gradually the Bibles were tolerated, Christian magazines were left lying around, and Dad was seen to pick them up for a read if he thought that no one was looking!

While some opposition starts early, is long term, even violent, it's not insurmountable. As we've already seen the Devil is a beaten enemy! We don't know how long the Thessalonian opposition lasted, but long or short, the Christians knew where they were going. Paul and Timothy had prepared them well.

DIRECT ATTACKS

Of course, as we've already noted, the Devil also knows how to attack us directly, in addition to using people. Thoughts, doubts, temptations – they're all part of his direct onslaught.

- He knows how to hit us hard:
  'Call yourself a Christian . . . ?'
  'You haven't got what it takes to follow Christ . . .'
- And when you've failed:
  'You're a write-off . . .'
  'You'll never kick that habit . . .'

'And so you've lied again . . .'
'You weren't genuine from the start . . .'
- Or he tries another tack:
'God doesn't love you . . .'
'Don't throw your life away . . .'
'Get out and enjoy yourself . . .'

Have you got around to recognising Satan's voice? You can justifiably tell him to go to hell – that's where he belongs.

So, it's a battle; one that starts the moment we trust Jesus as our Saviour. No wonder Paul tried hard to get back to those Thessalonian Christians. His sense of urgency comes out as he writes: '. . . out of our intense longing we made every effort to see you. For we wanted to come to you – certainly I, Paul, did, again and again – but Satan stopped us.' (1 Thessalonians 2:18). However, Timothy did a tremendous job.

OPPOSITION SHAPES OUR LIVES

It's clear that opposition helps to shape our Christian lives, positively as well as negatively.

Let's face up to those negative possibilities first. Janette was a house group member.

'I've decided to keep my mouth shut at work,' she rather hesitantly confided when the subject of witnessing came up. 'Well, no one's interested,' she went on, 'and I could never think of the right thing to say. People just throw one question after another at you, and I just don't know the answers. I suppose I don't really know the Bible well enough.'

Marion had a similar problem: the secretary with

whom she shared the office was older, divorced, and was absorbed with the problem of bringing up a family.

'She just isn't on my wavelength,' concluded Marion, 'I haven't got a clue how I'd cope with the mess she's in. So what can *I* say?'

Both Janette and Marion wrestled with feelings of inadequacy, fear, ignorance, inexperience. Faced with our own felt inability to speak effectively for Christ there's the risk of retreating into silence. Our commitment remains a well-kept secret.

But why give up? Defeat isn't inevitable. Timothy's role in strengthening and encouraging the young Christians in Thessalonica was to equip them to deal with difficulties. Remind yourself of those verses again:

> 'We sent Timothy . . . to strengthen and encourage
> you in your faith, so that no-one would be unsettled
> by these trials. You know quite well that we were
> destined for them. In fact, when we were with you,
> we kept telling you that we would be persecuted.
> And it turned out that way, as you well know.'
> 1 Thessalonians 3:2–4

The result? They knew what they believed and weren't afraid to share it.

So how are we to cope with opposition?

● Recognise its origin – Satan. We can resist him in the name of Jesus, standing firm in our faith.
● Know God's word. That's how Jesus defeated the Devil (Matthew 4:1–11). Remember Janette's weakness. We need to be able to give a reason for our faith (1 Peter 3:15). We may not be well-equipped initially, but regular Bible study in our church fellowship and at a personal level will steadily meet the need. Getting to

know God's word gradually builds up an understanding that's invaluable for responding to questions and dealing with problems.

• Recognise your fear, and stand, relying not on your abilities but on Jesus and his Spirit.

• Don't be afraid to share your testimony of what God has done for you personally. That's real, and no one can take away your experience. They may ridicule, but they can't destroy the truth, and they may well come to believe. That's often how people are won for Christ.

• Don't compromise, but stick with what you know is right. The old excuse, 'Everybody does it', doesn't let you off the hook. If you compromise, you've lost your Christian distinctiveness and people will ignore what you say. Remember Shah. Over a long period he was finally brought to compromise and failure.

• Keep your cool. If you get hot under the collar and retaliate you've lost – even if you win the argument.

• Be kind, patient and forgiving. Silently holding a grudge because of the rough ride you're given will undermine your determination to live for Christ. Work on Jesus' words: 'Love your enemies . . .' (Matthew 5: 44).

• Keep praying. Jesus went on to say, 'and pray for those who persecute you.'

• Share your situation and needs with Christian friends – a house group can be a good place. We can always benefit from others' experiences, learning from the way they have handled situations. And we can pray for each other.

• If you fail, it's not the end. Confess it to the Lord who knows and understands. Get up and go on. Shah finally did so and he won his battle with Satan.

• Don't forget to read regularly Christian books and

booklets. Ask your church leader for suggestions. A good Christian bookshop can also give useful ideas.

The Thessalonians remain a good example of overcoming opposition and Paul's comment in chapter 1, verse 8 says it all: 'The Lord's message rang out from you not only in Macedonia and Achaia – your faith in God has become known everywhere.'

Opposition certainly didn't dampen the Thessalonians' spirits. They got on the move, sharing the good news, covering much of Greece and parts of modern Albania and what was Yugoslavia. No matter what, spread the good news through what you say and the way you live. Shah was contacted for Christ when a man braved the hostility of Multan and spoke about Jesus in the crowded streets of the city. Josephine believed because of a Billy Graham radio broadcast and brought her sisters to know Jesus in the face of persistent opposition at home. Opposition doesn't have the last word. God does.

GOD GIVES JOY

And, what's more, God gives a bonus. Even in opposition he can give us joy! See what Paul writes:

> '. . . in spite of severe suffering you welcomed the message with the joy given by the Holy Spirit.'
> 1 Thessalonians 1:6

Joy came to those early Christians, as it does to us, through the Holy Spirit who was at work in their lives. Paul spells out the facts in Galatians 5:22, 'The fruit of the Spirit is love, joy . . .' Let's remind ourselves that we can experience the Spirit's joy not only when everything is plain sailing, but even when life is tough.

Jesus knew this full well. Teaching his disciples as they sat together on the mountainside above Lake Galilee, he said:

> 'Happy are those who are persecuted because they do what God requires; the Kingdom of heaven belongs to them!
>
> 'Happy are you when people insult you and persecute you and tell all kinds of evil lies against you because you are my followers. By happy and glad, for a great reward is kept for you in heaven.'
>
> *Matthew 5:10–12*, Good News Bible

Joy from persecution? Really? Well, some of us discovered the truth of Jesus' words one Sunday afternoon on the busy streets of Lahore, Pakistan. We were sharing the good news about Jesus with any who were prepared to stop and listen. The crowd thickened. Finally, the police arrived and we were removed to the local police station.

'I understand you were creating a disturbance in the bazaar,' stated the officer. 'What have you got to say about it?'

'We were giving out Christian literature,' we told him, 'and talking about the Lord Jesus Christ. People crowded around us. And many wanted to find out more. Others didn't like what we had to say.'

As we went on, explaining why we were there and who Jesus is, we experienced a deep-down joy which the Spirit gives – the joy of being Jesus' witnesses, knowing he was with us, helping us. We discovered again that thinking about hostile crowds and individuals could make us feel weak at the knees – and the police station with its cells wasn't very inviting! But with the act of sharing the good news came a joy which no one could take away. Have you ever experienced it: that mixture of apprehension and joy, fear and happiness? That's how it was that Sunday afternoon.

The location's not important, neither are the details. You'll get a reaction wherever you share the good news about Jesus. It could be London's Leicester Square, Bradford, Birmingham, Berlin, Bratislava, Budapest – or your own home town, in your office or in a visiting programme from your church. And if it's tough, we'll know we are one with the Thessalonians, one with Jesus and one with Paul, too, who shared his experience with the Corinthian Christians: 'I am greatly encouraged; in all our troubles my joy knows no bounds' (2 Corinthians 7:4). That's a staggering thought. Most of us have a long way to go before we catch up with the apostle!

None of us, of course, goes out looking for trouble, opposition or persecution, but as we face it, it will be a means in God's hand to help us grow – slowly, sometimes painfully, yet joyously – making us more like Jesus. That's something to remember next time the Devil gets at you!

3
GROW IN LOVE

The alarm rang relentlessly. Three-thirty is not the best time to get up on a cold winter's morning; it was still pitch dark! Hidayat rolled reluctantly out of bed. Half an hour later he was pedalling his bike towards one of Lahore's sweeper colonies. It was a filthy area, the home of a group of sweepers who served that part of the city. On this particular morning Hidayat wanted to get there early before the men left for work. There was no main drainage at that time, so emptying out and cleaning latrines required the sweepers to visit their clients' homes daily from around five o'clock. That was the best time; before the majority got up and were disturbed by the stench the cleaners created.

Sweeper colonies left outsiders with mixed feelings. The people were illiterate and lived in broken-down hovels. Open refuse carts would stand around their shacks throughout the day. The area was disease-ridden and filled with flies and stench. Children played among the oxen and the refuse carts. Some of the men were on drugs. They were poor and despised. Nobody cared about them. But there was Hidayat, pastor of his local church, and Hidayat did care – you could call it love. Nothing but love would get him out of bed at three-thirty in the morning to arrive at their little colony just after four, and to share with them the love of the Lord Jesus Christ, to talk over their problems, to do what he could to help alleviate their difficulties. Hidayat was there, again and again, and they loved Hidayat. There weren't many people like him who were willing to take time and talk through their difficulties, to try to help the babies who were ill, to take care of problems as they arose. He would watch over them, be their friend. He was love in action.

Shift the scene to the streets of London or any of our major towns or cities: drop-outs in their cardboard boxes, rejects, drug addicts. Get out on the streets, not to stare but to care, and discover that love is the only enduring motive. It drives Mother Teresa and her colleagues in Calcutta. It compelled General Booth, who founded the Salvation Army, and impels thousands who have followed him. And what but love can send men and women effectively to the world of Islam, to followers of the Buddha or to devotees of western materialistic greed – and keep them on the job, expending their lives as they share the good news about Jesus?

LOVE STARTS WITH GOD

Love, as we see it in people, is powerful and effective, but love starts with God. We discover this in 1 Thessalonians 1:4, where Paul writes: 'Brothers loved by God, we know that he has chosen you.' God's love is the primary reality and motivation. All love flows from him; to the Thessalonians, to Hidayat, and to us. In

41

verse 5 we discover that the good news, about the love of God, came to the Thessalonians verbally, but also with life-changing power. God was at work among them, using Paul, to bring them the experience of his love. His love was made real, too, through his Holy Spirit's activity, and it came to them, we are told, with deep conviction. Let's read those verses again:

> 'Brothers loved by God, we know that he has chosen you, because our gospel came to you not simply with words, but also with power, with the Holy Spirit, and with deep conviction.'

God has never loved or chosen people because they were wonderful. That was true of his own people the Jews. We find way back in the Old Testament in Deuteronomy 7:6–8 that he tells the people through Moses:

> 'The LORD your God has chosen you out of all the peoples on the face of the earth to be his people, his treasured possession. The LORD did not set his affection on you and choose you because you were more numerous than other peoples, for you were the fewest of all peoples. But it was because the LORD loved you.'

That's true of all those to whom the Lord comes. In 1 Timothy 1:15, 16 Paul calls himself 'the worst of sinners'. Yet the Lord loved him. And writing about us in Romans 5:8 he tells us: 'God demonstrates his own love for us in this: While we were still sinners, Christ died for us.'

LOVE GOD IN RETURN

This amazing love calls for a response, one that is simple, obvious, yet demanding – that we should love God in return. In this letter to the Thessalonians there's no explicit call to love God. They already did. This responding love was demonstrated, not only by Paul in his bringing the good news, but by the Thessalonians as well in the way they responded to the gospel (Acts 17:4–10) and went on to live out God's love among themselves. Actions really do speak louder than words.

LOVE IS A TOP PRIORITY

Underlining the practical nature of love, Paul goes on to remind them how vital it is. They were surrounded by problems, difficulties and opposition, as we have already seen. So he says to them in chapter 5, verse 8:

> 'Let us be self-controlled, putting on faith and love as a breastplate, and the hope of salvation as a helmet.'

This trio of faith, love and hope reminds us of 1 Corinthians 13:13. And of these, love is described there as being 'the greatest'. Here were people who had to take love, along with faith and hope, as effective armour with which to arm themselves against the attacks of the Devil. Perhaps under Satanic attack love might not seem to be the most appropriate of weapons, but it's there at the forefront of God's armoury. Love is effective in touching the lives of those whom Satan may stir up against us.

Love is basic. Love is essential. The Lord Jesus said

that the first commandment for each of us is: 'Love the Lord your God with all your heart and with all your soul and with all your mind' (Matthew 22:37).

LOVE IS EXPRESSED IN ACTION

This love isn't a gooey sentimentalism, or something that might surface only in a church service, a time of worship or in prayer. This is a love – as we're discovering – which expresses itself in a whole range of experiences and actions. We have already noted its effectiveness as armour in conflict, but that's just one aspect of it's activity. Paul recognised it as energising the Thessalonians' commitment to Christ, motivating them to serve him without counting the cost; Paul refers to their 'labour prompted by love (1:3). God is more impressed by what we do in expressing our love, than by a million words that we might say to him about it. It was what Hidayat *did*, in getting out on a winter's morning in Lahore and cycling to the sweeper encampment, that demonstrated his love. They wouldn't have been so convinced had he just told them, 'I do love you, I care about you and I'll pray for you', yet had never gone out to their dilapidated hovels where they lived, never got alongside them to help them where they hurt. That's how we discover what love really is.

• Put together a list of people who particularly need loving in your fellowship, and for each note down the way in which that love could be expressed – there will be different acts of love for different people. Make that list a spur for action.

LOVE WITHOUT STRINGS ATTACHED

The Thessalonians had seen this kind of love being worked out in Paul. Men and women, boys and girls saw it being worked out in Hidayat's life. It has to be love without strings attached and without reserve. Paul, when he writes to the Corinthians in 2 Corinthians 5:14, sums it up in four significant words: 'Christ's love compels us.' That's enough.

Take a look at Paul's track record. It was the 'no-strings-attached-love' that sent him to Thessalonica. He had been beaten up in Philippi immediately before setting out for this Thessalonian project. We read about it in Acts 16. First, there's the experience of throwing out the evil spirit from the slave-girl who was being used as a fortune teller by her owners. Verse 19 records how they seized Paul and Silas and dragged them into the market place to face the authorities. Then we see how the crowd joined in attacking them, and that the magistrates ordered them to be stripped and beaten. After the flogging they were thrown into prison where the jailor locked them in an inner cell and fastened their feet in the stocks.

With the background of these experiences, Paul very soon afterwards found himself in Thessalonica, but there wasn't a moment's hesitation. Christ's compelling love urged him forward. Acts 17:2, 3 records his first efforts in the synagogue, where on three Sabbaths, he explained to the Jews that Jesus was the Messiah. And when some believed he set about nurturing them. 1 Thessalonians 2:7, 8 describes the love that kept him going. He writes:

> 'As apostles of Christ we could have been a burden
> to you, but we were gentle among you, like a

mother caring for her little children. We loved you so much that we were delighted to share with you not only the gospel of God but our lives as well, because you had become so dear to us.'

NOT A BURDEN

His love was being worked out, and we see what was involved. Love didn't want to become a burden. 'As apostles of Christ,' he writes 'we could have been a burden.' But determined to support themselves, he goes on, 'we worked night and day in order not to be a burden to anyone while we preached the gospel of God to you.' Love refuses to be a burden, and it finds a way of avoiding it.

True love takes the load off people and doesn't increase it. Our loving activity can sometimes leave those we seek to help feeling burdened: a word, an emphasis can be counter-productive. Take Anne, for example, trying her best to help some of the older church members. Quickly she picks up the phone, organising another busy day: 'Sorry, Jane, I can only give you half an hour in the garden this morning. I haven't forgotten your shopping, and I'll try to fit it in tomorrow, but I've got to get John into hospital by two o'clock.' Anne means well, but she's getting the wrong message across. Jane, struggling with angina, now has the added burden of feeling she's a drag.

There are quite a few ways of becoming a burden! It's a challenge to discover the secret of giving ourselves totally to the 'love' in hand without reference to other concerns. The impression that 'I've got all the time in the world for you right now' is the skill to cultivate.

Love finds a way – but as Paul discovered, it can be costly.

GENTLE YET STRONG

There was a gentleness about Paul's love that the Thessalonians must have been quick to recognise. The phrase he uses: 'gentle . . . like a mother caring . . .' was used literally to describe a mother breastfeeding her baby. It was this gentle, loving tenderness which motivated Paul in all his relationships with the Thessalonian Christians.

Perhaps that was why his evangelism and church planting was so effective: people knew from personal experience that here was a man prepared, not only to stand up and preach, but to share every aspect of his life with them. He gave his time – sacrificially – as he worked 'night and day' earning his own living, as well as teaching, counselling and nurturing. At the same time he endured the ongoing hatred of the local Jewish community, always ready to stir up opposition. His emotions were torn, too, as he saw them won by the love of Christ and immediately plunged into suffering for him. It was all part of a life-sharing commitment, stimulated by a compelling motivation – '. . . you had become so dear to us.'

Paul is not only a mother to the Thessalonian Christians, he becomes their father as well, as he writes in verses 11 and 12:

> 'For you know that we dealt with each of you as a
> father deals with his children, encouraging,
> comforting and urging you to live lives worthy of
> God.'

So Paul's love is being worked out in a variety of ways, and chapter 1, verse 5 sums it up well; 'You know how we lived among you for your sake.' He lived out his love 'for their sake.' Paul's way of loving is something to grow into.

LOVE CREATES LOVE

Friends of ours wanted to foster a teenage girl, Kay. Kay had spent most of her life in institutions and residential homes. She had been fostered before, and it hadn't worked out, for no one could really handle her. But Jan and David felt drawn to Kay, and wanted to help. They took her into their home and it was a riot. Plates were thrown and smashed. She would fly into violent fits of fury. Abuse was the order of the day. But David and Jan loved Kay, and wanted to help. With patience, care and understanding they stayed alongside her day after day.

During that period, David took home a pictorial New Testament. Kay dipped into it, finding the pictures of Jesus attractive, but it was the scenes of him on the cross which really grabbed her heart. It wasn't long before Kay and Jan wrote out a prayer together, and very simply Kay put her trust in Jesus. In his great love God gave her a 'picture' – a vision of Jesus coming down from the cross and giving her a wonderful hug. She had found someone who really loved her.

The preceding weeks and months had been preparing Kay. She hadn't known much about Jesus, but she had seen without realising it a great deal of his love in David and Jan. Their love had made the introduction.

Soon afterwards David had to go away to a conference. Just as he was leaving the house Kay ran up to him, put her arms around his neck, and hugged and kissed him as she said goodbye. So far as David knew, that was the first expression of real love that she had ever made. Kay had come to recognise a love she had never previously experienced – the love of Jesus living in David and Jan.

There came a time when, for various reasons, Kay had to go away. David and Jan's hearts ached, wondering what would happen to her. In her ups and downs Kay had problems. She had joys, too. It was a fantastic experience after some months when David met her again, to be invited out by Kay to an evening meal, and at that meal to meet someone whom she had been able to introduce to Jesus Christ. Love was beginning to work itself out in practical ways in her daily life.

Paul knew the hurts and difficulties that love must handle. The devastating situation in Thessalonica forced him to leave abruptly. We read about it in chapter 2, verse 17. Though for different reasons, he must have felt rather like Jan and David when they had to part with Kay. He writes:

> 'Brothers, when we were torn away from you for a short time (in person, not in thought), out of our intense longing we made every effort to see you.'

But his efforts were fruitless. He did have, however, the joy of knowing that their love was beginning to grow. He'd already experienced that, as we've seen, when they sent him off to Berea in the middle of the night, so that he could carry on the work to which God had called him. But he desperately wanted to be with them again to help them, so that they might develop. That was love, working itself out in practice.

It's significant that love generates or gives birth to love. That's what was happening in Kay, and it was happening, too, in those Christian sweepers in the colony in Lahore. It happens again and again, for our hearts respond to love and kindness. It may start with an expression of gratitude, and gradually deepen as we respond to the on-going love of the person who comes to us.

On our television screens we've seen the devastating effects of widespread flooding, particularly in Bangladesh. Pakistan has had its fair share of flooding, too. Some years ago there was a massive flood around the city of Lahore, and out in a village called Missankala a group of Christians was totally cut off. Almost the entire village had been submerged by the water. After three days, waiting for it to subside, three of us set off for Missankala. Leading the way was Hidayat the pastor. Very few supplies could be carried; we had to wade through water, sometimes up to our chests. There were dead buffaloes caught up in the railway line we were trying to follow. Finally, after wading for about three miles, we got to the village. On our heads we had carried little packets of tea, sugar, rice and wheat flour – gifts from our church for their friends in this devastated village. The amount of food we had brought was small, and it certainly couldn't meet everyone's needs. But, it said one thing – 'We love you, we care about you.' Love that was expressed in little bags of rice, was met by those isolated Christians with love that said 'There's nothing that we can do right now, except to say thank you. But we love you. We know that you care, for we've seen the evidence.'

That same attitude of reciprocating love had steadily developed in Thessalonica; seen first in Paul himself as he lived among them. They knew from his motherly and fatherly care how deeply he loved them. We've read about it in chapter 2, verses 6, 8 and 12. They knew about his agony at being torn away from them; we've seen it in chapter 2, verse 17. And they loved Paul in return. That was the tremendous news that Timothy was able to bring back to him when he caught up with the apostle in Corinth. Paul refers to it in chapter 3, verse 6, where he writes:

> 'Timothy has just now come to us from you and has brought good news about your faith and love. He has told us that you always have pleasant memories of us and that you long to see us, just as we also long to see you.'

There was that mutual love between them. Paul's love had touched them deeply. For both it had been costly – both the demands and the effort invested had been great.

WORK AT LOVING

What's your experience? Your local church or fellowship group may be warm and caring. Christians have loved you, stuck with you through a whole range of experiences, shared in your sorrows and difficulties as well as your joys. Their love has found a response in your heart. You love, you help, you care – and the circle of your love is growing.

But perhaps all this fails to reflect your experience. You don't feel loved, but find yourself on the fringe. So far as you know, when you are absent, you're never missed, for no one ever asks where you've been. That's a problem; not all groups reflect the Thessalonian model. What is the answer? Does one solution lie in actively loving and getting involved yourself with Christians in the fellowship? That might well generate in them a love which responds to yours. That's how love grows, both in us, and in those we love. Love has to be worked at. And that's not always easy.

Often we find that the further some people are away from us, the easier it is to love them. That can be true of our own church members – easier to love when they're away on holiday! True, too, of Muslims or Hindus. We can love them as they are, two, three, seven thousand miles away, but we don't want them too near. If they come to live in our street, love may wear a bit thin. It's easier to give to famine relief or a disaster fund than it is to meet needy people on their doorstep down the road. So it's in the close-up situations, when we're close enough to feel the prickles, close enough to see the warts, that love is challenged. We're tempted to back off: they're just too awkward, too selfish, too arrogant. Love is needed right there – and it's not easy.

There was Bert. Difficult to love some would have said. By the time he was introduced to the church by his son, he was well over sixty and set in his ways. As everyone soon found out, Bert had been a gunner in the army. As an 8th Army 'desert rat', he'd fought his way across North Africa and through Italy. What he didn't know about guns wasn't worth knowing, as everyone soon discovered. Bert was a born survivor, tough as they come, bit of a know-all, ready to put everyone right. Much of the time Bert was suffered rather than loved. But David loved him and led him to Christ. A transformation started – not quickly enough for some! Gradually his strong self-centredness and self-assertion softened. There was a growing concern for others. Bert was great with his hands and the church property, with the grounds, soon showed the signs of his practical skills. It was perhaps knocking on people's doors in the outreach programme when Bert enjoyed himself most. While his blunt, direct approach made some of his friends cringe, he was effective, and at least one woman owed her conversion to Bert's forthright style. Even so, when Bert let himself loose on a house group – and he rarely missed a session – his unwitting dominance threatened even his house group leader's ingenuity! Bert was loved, warts and all, and his uninhibited affection won over otherwise resistant hearts during the fourteen or so years that he followed Christ. And if numbers attending his funeral are any indication, it was obvious that Bert had made his mark.

Love does transform, though the results don't always come quickly or easily. Fran was in her middle teens when she was first brought to the church youth group in desperation by her non-Christian parents. The school couldn't cope with her, psychiatric counselling had so far failed, and there was a record of suicide attempts. Fran was certainly a challenge to love, but loved she was, by young people who made room for her in their hearts and lives. They lived with her stealing and violent abuse. Love led to praying and careful planning. Fran was demanding. Counselling continued. The involvement consumed time, energy, patience and love. Sometimes progress has almost been matched by setbacks. But progress there is: she's working, though holding down a job isn't easy; now she has a flat of her own, and she's discovering a great capacity to love others.

Kay, Bert and Fran come as vivid reminders of those around us. The temptation is to concentrate on those who readily respond, and to leave the rest to others: people who have more time, more patience, greater counselling skills. The trouble is that those 'others' might just not be around, and God wants to love through *you*. Loving isn't always easy, and it can be rejected. Yet that's not reason for quitting.

NO LIMIT TO LOVE

Take a look at 1 Thessalonians 3:12, where Paul says to those Christians:

> 'May the Lord make your love increase and overflow for each other and for everyone else, just as ours does for you.'

And he goes on to emphasise the point in chapter 4, verses 9, 10:

> 'Now about brotherly love we do not need to write to you, for you yourselves have been taught by God to love each other. And in fact, you do love all the brothers throughout Macedonia. Yet we urge you, brothers, to do so more and more.'

If that Thessalonian church was anything like yours or mine, there must have been people in it who weren't easy to love. Yet Paul makes no distinction; he emphasises that their love should increase and overflow for each other, and for everyone else. So, do you find it difficult to love? There's hope here, because, as we've just seen, Paul makes the point that it's the *Lord* who can make their love increase and overflow. Left to ourselves we may well find it difficult to go on loving, but with his help it can increase and overflow in a wonderful way.

Paul's encouragement to love and the encouragement that comes to you and me is found, not in our innate ability to love, but in God himself. That's certainly encouraging! So if, under pressure, you feel that love's running out; that it's just not possible to go on loving, remind yourself that you have a loving teacher. No, not just Paul, though his example is amazing, the real teacher is God – Father, Son and Holy Spirit. So Paul emphasises in chapter 4, verse 9: '. . . you yourselves have been taught by God to love each other.' He is the one who first of all, as we saw at the beginning of this chapter, moved out in love toward us (1:4). He is the one who sent his Son to love and die for us. He is the one who 'has poured out his love into our hearts by the Holy Spirit, whom he has given us' (Romans 5:5). And the fruit of the Spirit is first of all love (Galatians 5:22). So be encouraged!

It's on these grounds that Paul makes his appeal to go on loving: 'We urge you, brothers, to do so more and more' (4:10).

LOVE GETS US MOVING

The unlimited love to which Paul refers reaches out, not only to 'each other', but to 'everyone else' (3:12). It's the supreme motivation for outreach and evangelism. Notice the example and incentive Paul gives: 'just as ours does for you.' So the Thessalonians reached out and touched their own city. But far beyond that. Remember the record of 1:8: 'The Lord's message rang out from you in Macedonia and Achaia.' Love 'for each other and for everyone else' took them hundreds of miles over the eastern Mediterranean.

Where is love directing your local church, and where do you fit into the strategy and programme?

● It can begin with a map of the local area, breaking down the district into manageable sections for the church to visit, house by house.

● Visiting teams will be needed. Rather than leave the outreach to just a few in the church, think about the possibility of encouraging the house groups – if you have them – to take on the task turn by turn over a set period of weeks or months.

● Arrange prayer sessions to cover outreach opportunities.

● Set up training sessions for outreach, using the Bible Society's 'Person to Person' video. Write to Bible Society, Stonehill Green, Westlea, Swindon, Wilts SN5 7DG.

● Organise the follow-up of interested contacts.

● Investigate the possibility of visiting old people's homes.

● Join a 'March for Jesus'. The Evangelical Alliance can provide information. Write to Whitefield House, 186 Kennington Park Road, London SE11 4BT. Telephone 071–582 0228.

● Arrange special outreach days – Saturdays are probably the best time – for literature distribution in specified locations in your town. If available, off-street shopping precincts are good venues. Special literature can be prepared, both evangelistic and leaflets giving information about your church, its location and activities. This outreach could be shared with other local churches.

• Investigate the possibilities of outreach by young people to young people – either on the streets or through other organised events.

• Look at the possibility of developing social work within the community. Fran Beckett's valuable book *Called to Action* (published by HarperCollins) is a mine of information.

• Parent and Toddler groups are invaluable, providing contacts which would otherwise be difficult to make.

• Consider the use of individuals' homes where you can: invite neighbours for a meal, watch a video, meet an interesting personality, hold coffee mornings, book parties, craft evenings. These are all useful bridge-building activities.

• All these ideas are just 'starters' to stimulate thinking, so why not set up a 'buzz-group' to discover a range of activities which your particular fellowship can get off the ground?

• Make sure that everything is done only with the cooperation of the church leaders. Otherwise there could be chaos!

• In addition to your local map, line up the maps of Europe, Africa, Asia, China and beyond. The world's a big place and still needs to hear the good news about Jesus. Invest in a copy of *Operation World* published by STL and obtainable through Christian bookshops. This book is packed with a whole range of information and statistics, with specific needs noted for prayer and action. Order magazines produced by organisations committed to Christian work overseas. For example,

Interserve produce 'Go', providing insights into much of the Muslim world, Nepal and other areas. (Obtainable from 325 Kennington Road, London SE11 4QH.) The Evangelical Missionary Alliance can provide information covering a wide range of Christian groups involved in overseas mission. Contact them at Whitefield House, 186 Kennington Park Road, London SE11 4BT, Telephone 071–735 0421.

In these ways – and through many others – Christ's love can motivate our prayers and actions, sending us, like Paul and the Thessalonians, to a world which needs desperately to meet with Jesus Christ. Let his love get to work.

LOVE YOUR LEADERS

Love God, love one another, love others in all their diversity throughout our land and beyond. Is that it? Not quite. Paul identifies another group: love your leaders. He writes about them in chapter 5, verses 12,13:

> 'Now we ask you, brothers, to respect those who work hard among you, who are over you in the Lord and who admonish you. Hold them in the highest regard in love because of their work. Live in peace with each other.'

They are the ones who in our churches are often taken for granted, frequently neglected. They are the hard-worked pastors, elders, ministers, youth workers. But, of course, aren't *they* supposed to do the loving, and to be examples? Of course, they are – but not exclusively.

I have a friend, Colin, who all too often shows signs of wear and tear. He's a pastor. His hours are spent in counselling, visiting, teaching. There are dedications, and baptisms. He has marriages to perform, funerals to take and a pile of administration to take care of. He needs to spend time in prayer and in preparation. He needs to foster his own spiritual life. And he has to care, too, for his own family. And yet Colin's criticised when he fails – actual or imagined failure – sometimes it's just that he's failed to meet the expectations of individuals in the fellowship. And that kind of criticism is hard to take when time and again you have loved and cared and tried to do what is right and fair. Colin, like those leaders to whom Paul refers, works hard, or 'labours' – that's the word Paul uses on a number of occasions, both in this and other letters. The word itself means 'to work to the point of exhaustion' – total fatigue, if you like. There it is in verse 12: 'Brothers, respect those who work hard among you.'

They are the ones who seem to wear themselves out in the fellowship: caring, loving. They need special treatment. Paul's advice (5:12,13) provides guidelines for shaping our attitudes to the leaders God has given us.

● Respect them, for they are God's servants in a position of responsibility, with responsibilities that are sometimes difficult to fulfil. One of them is *admonishing*. Theirs is a tough job! Congratulating, encouraging – that's attractive and relatively easy, but admonishing isn't exactly the pastor's first choice. The Good News Bible helps us to understand what lies behind the word, translating 'those who admonish you' as 'those . . . who guide and instruct you in the Christian life.' That leaves room for both positive and negative instruction; it includes both congratulations and rebukes. Both are needed and both can be accepted when we know that our leaders are motivated by love.

● Regard them, hold them in the *highest regard in love* because of their work – the things they do day in day out, at all hours, anticipating and responding to a multitude of needs. Check over the list of Colin's activities, and then note down the actions and involvement of those who work in your own fellowship.

● Love them, remembering that love is best expressed in action. It's more than a warm, kindly feeling. Another list might be appropriate here, setting out your acts of love for your leaders: ways, for example, of helping to meet their own needs – needs for relaxation, needs in their family, ways of lightening their load.

● Live in peace. Leaders' loads would certainly be lightened if we regularly took on board Paul's final piece of advice in verse 13, 'Live in peace with each other.' Disagreements, quarrels, back-biting, slander, however subtle, are all factors that destroy peace and tear a fellowship apart. How much time does your pastor have to spend mending relationships? The leader's load is lightened when we truly take to heart Paul's prayer that our love should 'increase and overflow for each other'. That's the path to peace. And if we think we're doing pretty well, then he says with good reason, 'Yet we urge you, brothers, do so more and more'!

LOVE TILL IT HURTS

But before we leave the subject, let's take a further look at this word 'labour', or 'hard work', for, in fact, it applies to all of us, not just to our leaders. Each one of us is called to love until it hurts, spending ourselves in order to help others. The noun comes in this letter three times; in 1:3; 2:9 and 3:5. The verb is used in 5:12. And as we look at these verses, we see clearly how hard work characterised Paul; hard work that was motivated by love. Take a look again at chapter 2, verses 7, 9, where Paul writes:

> 'As apostles of Christ we could have been a burden to you, but we were gentle among you, like a mother caring for her little children. We loved you so much that we were delighted to share with you not only the gospel of God but our lives as well, because you had become so dear to us.'

Then, he goes on immediately to add:

> 'Surely you remember, brothers, our toil and hardship; we worked night and day in order not to be a burden to anyone . . .'

Paul was a tent-maker by trade, and along with his tent-making he was involved in teaching, in pastoral care, nurturing the new Christians, sharing his life with them. 'Toil' translates the same Greek word rendered in other parts of the letter as 'labour' or 'hard work' or 'efforts'. That was 'work to the point of exhaustion'. And undoubtedly that's how it left the apostle – exhausted. Add to that the hours he spent in prayer. Note chapter 3 verse 10: 'Day and night we pray most earnestly . . .'

No wonder he felt devastated when opposition forced him to leave for Berea. It seemed possible that in spite of all his exhausting efforts the work in Thessalonica would collapse. So we read in chapter 3, verse 5:

> 'I was afraid that in some way the tempter might have tempted you and our efforts [our labour, our hard work – it's the same word] might have been useless.'

Enter into the intensity of the apostle's love for the Thessalonian Christians: love that urged him to nurture them like a deeply caring mother, love that drove him to share his life in teaching, interceding, and all the time earning his own living. That's the stature of Paul! He worked hard, and expressed his love in that way.

It's not surprising that Paul's love and sacrificial service deeply influenced the Thessalonian believers. We've already seen how love creates love, but the fact to note here, however, is the *extent* to which the love grew. The same attitude, the same hard work or labour which we have seen in Paul's life now characterised *them*. So in chapter 1, verse 3 Paul uses that significant word again; this time to describe the Thessalonians, 'We continually remember before our God and Father . . . your *labour prompted by love*.'

These men and women who had seen so much love in the life of the apostle were similarly motivated to live as he lived. The exhaustion Paul experienced, as he lovingly poured out his strength for them, sparked off the same response in their own spiritual lives. And that's how it should be. It was a love that grew and got things done. That's what impelled Hidayat to go out in the early morning to meet those sweepers. It was that effective love that embraced Bert and Fran, transforming their lives.

It's a love to be worked out at a local level in our own churches, in our families, and in our work situations where we seek to live for the Lord Jesus Christ. And it's a love that is meant to grow and develop, reproducing itself again and again as others are captured by its embrace and are liberated to love in return.

● How far have you gone in the process of loving? What steps do you need to take for that love to increase, to grow and overflow?

4

GROW IN COMMITMENT

Commitment is usually expressed in action. It begins, of course, in our hearts and minds, it involves our faith and our love, and it's expressed in endurance, the way we press on and refuse to give up.

Miss Wilkins and Mrs Austin came into that category. They belonged to a church in south London and, like many churches, it was fairly empty. For years, they had been without a minister, and there seemed very little hope of getting one. But Miss Wilkins and Mrs Austin prayed about it, and their prayers probably extended over something like a decade. As they prayed, they were specific, asking that God would send them the person who was really needed. They prayed about the many people who surrounded the church, the boys and girls, with no attractive Sunday School to go to. They prayed for the Christians who needed to be built up and strengthened. But who would want to come to a church which was so empty, and apparently without any real prospects of growth? God, however, heard their prayers as they committed themselves to bringing these needs before him day by day, and God sent his own man. Before many months were out, the church began to fill, the pews finally were crowded, and they had to bring in chairs to put down the aisles. People turned to Jesus Christ, and it became a growing, thriving community. It seems from the evidence that two women, in their commitment to prayer, to see needs met, were largely responsible.

We can see this happening at every level and with every age group. A probation officer, also in the London area, spent his time getting alongside young offenders, helping them over a wide range of their experiences, being a friend, and when appropriate sharing with them what the Lord Jesus could do. The day came when a young client, armed with a bottle of ammonia, called – and Geoff the probation officer received it full in his face. It led to blindness, but not to the end of his commitment to those young people. Geoff kept on going.

GOD IS COMMITTED TO US

The greatest example of commitment, however, comes to us from God himself. He's committed to us in the fullest sense of the word, and he shows us how to be committed. As we've already seen, Paul reminds the Thessalonians that they are people whom God loves, whom he has chosen, and whom he will never let go. That commitment, of course, was supremely demonstrated when he sent Jesus Christ into this world, not just for the Thessalonian Christians, but for the whole human race. And the God who was committed to the extent that he sent his only Son, is the one who doesn't let people slip through his fingers. His help is guaranteed, no matter what we face. This was Paul's experi-

ence as he determined to serve God. He writes in 1
Thessalonians 2:2:

> 'We had previously suffered and been insulted in
> Philippi, as you know, but with the help of our God
> we dared to tell you his gospel in spite of strong
> opposition.'

The key words there seem to be – 'with the help of
our God'. He was the one who sustained Paul, was
completely committed to him, helping him day by day.
The Thessalonians went on to know that help as they,
like Paul, passed through times of opposition. It's been
experienced by Christians over the centuries, and we
can depend on it, too. God's commitment to us ranges
over every area of life. No situation or need is excluded.
This assurance proves a powerful incentive to hand over
our lives totally to him. So commitment becomes the
hallmark of Christian living; at least, that's what God
is looking for.

When we think about commitment it's helpful to
spell out just what areas of life are involved. We discover how our commitment is to be expressed – what
it involves. Let's look at some of these factors.

COMMITTED TO GOD

For us the most important area of commitment, of
course, is to God himself. When Jesus was asked what
was the most important commandment, he replied without any hesitation: 'Love the Lord your God with all
your heart and with all your soul and with all your
mind and with all your strength' (Mark 12:30). That's
a commitment which calls for the total involvement of

every fibre of our being – heart, soul, mind, strength. When we're committed in this way to God, we discover how to please him, to bring him joy. Paul mentions how these Thessalonians were to be committed in chapter 4, verse 1. He writes:

> '. . . we instructed you how to live in order to please God, as in fact you are living.'

It's in pleasing God that we show the depth of our commitment. Take a look, also, at 2 Timothy 2:3,4. There Paul is writing to Timothy, and just as Paul had told the Thessalonians that the great aim was to please God, so he spells it out in these verses to his young friend:

> 'Endure hardship with us like a good soldier of Christ Jesus. No-one serving as a soldier gets involved in civilian affairs – he wants to please his commanding officer.'

That single-mindedness in wanting to please God, will control every facet of our lives. It's the emphasis in 1 Thessalonians 2:12, where Paul reminds them how as a spiritual father he had encouraged, comforted and urged them 'to live lives worthy of God' – lives that would please him.

COMMITTED TO GOD'S WORD

Commitment to God himself is undoubtedly the first and most important priority for each one of us. But alongside that there is another strand of commitment. These Thessalonian Christians were committed to

God's word and its message. It had come to them – and it comes to us – as *good news*, a living word which spells it out with all the hope and certainty that we need. As we receive it, so we can share it. This was Paul's attitude, and opposition couldn't stop it. We've already seen in 2:2, how in spite of being hassled, beaten up and imprisoned in Philippi, he was able to record: '... *we dared to tell you his gospel* in spite of strong opposition.' So we read in chapter 1, verse 8 Paul's testimony about them: 'The Lord's message rang out from you not only in Macedonia and Achaia – your faith in God has become known everywhere.' There was no doubt about their commitment to the good news, God's living word.

It's a word then that has to be whole-heartedly accepted and obeyed. Paul underlines that in chapter 2, verse 13, where he writes:

> '... we also thank God continually because, when
> you received the word of God, which you heard
> from us, you accepted it not as the word of men, but
> as it actually is, the word of God, which is at work
> in you who believe.'

As that word worked in their lives, they became obedient men and women, getting the good news out to others.

Here is a word which comes with divine authority. This was something that Paul undoubtedly underlined, not only for Timothy, but for all those with whom he came in contact. He spells it out clearly in 2 Timothy 3:16, 17:

> 'All Scripture is God-breathed and is useful for
> teaching, rebuking, correcting and training in

righteousness, so that the man of God may be thoroughly equipped for every good work.'

So Scripture comes authoritatively and applies not only to areas of belief and teaching, but is also important for training in righteousness – in upright living – making us people of integrity, committed to doing whatever God requires. The question has to be asked: how do we respond to God's authoritative word? Do our belief and actions – our whole way of life – reflect a practical commitment to it? What effect does its authority have?

One day, in Scripture Union's London office, someone called at reception and asked to meet a staff member who could explain to him the word of God. We sat together, and he told me his story. As a Communist, he had gone to the Midlands to set up subversive cells in a number of factories. He booked into the hotel, went to his room, and he found on the bedside cupboard a Gideon Bible. His immediate reaction was to put it in the drawer, and shut it firmly. During the day he went to various factories. On returning to the hotel in the evening he had nothing to do, and for some reason opened that drawer, and took out the Gideon Bible. He read it. In the course of those few days that he spent in the Midlands God spoke to him through his word, and he trusted the Lord Jesus as his Saviour. Returning to London he shared his experience with his wife. She had an old, unread copy of the Bible, and they looked at it together. She turned to Christ as well. When he told the local Communist Party of the radical change that had taken place in his life, they threw him out. Not only so, they were evicted from their home. Two new Christians found themselves very much alone. As it happened, he worked near Scripture Union's office, and guessing that it might have something to do with 'holy Scripture', he came in that day and made his request. At the end of his story, he looked me straight in the eye and said: 'As a Communist, I did exactly what the Communist Party wanted me to do. I was wholly committed to them. Now I'm wholly committed to Christ. You know his word. Tell me what I should do, and I'll do it.'

Right from the outset, this man was committed to the Lord Jesus Christ and to God's powerful and authoritative word. And, with Christ's help and the guidance that word provided, his commitment was going to grow and develop. How does your commitment affect the way you live?

● One of the most important steps we can take after trusting Christ to save us, is to study his word. That's why Scripture Union has an extensive, daily Bible reading programme, designed to meet a wide range of personal needs and interests.

● Many churches have house groups which major on Bible study, providing a firm base for building our Christian lives. The group structure gives opportunities for discussion, when we can benefit from others' insights and develop our own. Such groups sometimes follow their church's own teaching programme. Alternatively, there is Scripture Union's *LifeBuilder* Bible study series, which is especially designed for this purpose.

If possible get involved in a study group, and most certainly organise your own times of personal Bible study. We can't be committed to God's word if we don't know or understand it. But as we study it and obey what it says, our commitment will develop. We'll find in that word all we need to know about God the Father, his Son and the Holy Spirit. We'll discover, too, God's guidelines for living, and we'll have a message we've proved to be true and which we can share with those around us. Be committed to the truth!

COMMITTED TO MY CALLING

We move on from commitment to God and his word, with its message, to the calling that God gives us. God has a purpose for each one of us, and he wants us to be committed to pursuing that purpose, until it's brought to completion.

As Paul went from place to place sharing the good news, he knew that this was God's calling for him. Note what he writes in chapter 2, verse 4:

> '. . . We speak as men approved by God to be entrusted with the gospel.'

That was God's call to Paul, and he gives us equally specific calls. First of all there's the call to follow him, to be like him, to obey him, to be committed in every way through the lives that we live. That's our calling. Paul refers to it in chapter 2, verse 12, where he says that as a spiritual father he had encouraged, comforted and urged them to live lives worthy of God. We've already looked at that passage. Now take on board the full impact of those three words, 'worthy of God'. That is what our lives are meant to be. The apostle enlarges on this in chapter 4, verse 7, where he writes:

> 'God did not call us to be impure but to live a holy life.'

71

Lives lived worthy of God, are lives which are holy, completely committed to him, given over to him, separate from evil and wrong. So, whatever other calling he may give us, it starts from this base; to be holy, living lives worthy of him. He will certainly go on to call us to be faithful witnesses in our families and at work. He may even call us, as he called Paul, to work full-time for him – as an evangelist, a Bible teacher, a pastor, a youth worker.

Paul found that in his commitment to his calling there were sometimes temptations – temptations to abuse it. He refers to this in chapter 2, verses 3–6, where he states clearly:

> '. . . The appeal we make does not spring from impure motives, nor are we trying to trick you.'

And he goes on:

> 'We are not trying to please men but God, who tests our hearts. You know we never used flattery, nor did we put on a mask to cover up greed – God is our witness. We were not looking for praise from men, not from you or anyone else.'

There was a single-mindedness about his commitment which refused to make personal capital out of what God had called him to do; to give in to impure motives, descending to flattery to build up his personal rating; greedy for money, status or praise. In Paul's day many were going around as itinerant preachers, making money out of those to whom they went, sponging on their followers who entertained them lavishly in their homes. Studiously avoiding all this, Paul makes it plain that rather than be a burden to the church he had worked to support himself (2:9).

We can abuse our calling. Paul's temptations may not be ours, but as we live for Jesus Christ, it's very likely that we shall have some in common with him. There may well be the desire to bring attention to ourselves, to be praised by others – to have wrong motives in a variety of ways. When we learn to be single-minded in the way we respond to God's call, we shall live more effectively for him.

Timothy is a good example of this. We find in chapter 3, verse 2 that Paul writes of him: 'We sent Timothy, who is our brother and God's fellow-worker in spreading the gospel of Christ, to strengthen and encourage you in your faith'. That describes Timothy well. There was no doubt about his commitment to God – 'God's fellow-worker' – and as a teacher and pastor; his commitment to the call he had received stands out clearly. Paul could trust him implicitly to strengthen and encourage those young Christians whom Paul had been forced to leave so abruptly. In 1 Corinthians 4:17 Paul sums it all up when he says about Timothy: 'he is faithful in the Lord'. So, whatever our calling, it's in terms of faithfulness that our commitment is going to be measured: faithful in the Lord, in our daily work, in the way we live at home, in every contact that we have. That's how our commitment will be demonstrated.

Think carefully about the calling God has for you.

• How would you define your calling at home: as a mother, father, son or daughter? How will your faithfulness to the Lord Jesus be expressed in those relationships?

- What about our work situations, our commitment to our employers, to colleagues and to the work itself on the one hand, coupled with our calling to live for Christ in all that we do?
- Has God got a role for you in your local fellowship or Christian Union? It might involve an evening each week, plus preparation time, visiting, following up contacts, praying, too. What is the cost of that commitment?
- Are there opportunities during holiday periods? Does your church run a holiday club for boys and girls with which you could help? Is God calling you to give part of your holiday to help with a Scripture Union beach mission or camp? They are hard work, but tremendous fun and deeply rewarding. Commitment has it costs and returns. Contact Scripture Union at 130 City Road, London EC1V 2NJ.
- How about being a Scripture Union church representative, promoting SU's Bible reading programmes and keeping everyone informed of the many ways in which SU can help the fellowship.
- There are great opportunities for short-term involvement overseas. Interserve has many openings in this area and also runs an 'On Track' programme which provides opportunities for both students and graduates with a variety of skills, including medicine, education, and engineering, for example. There could be a call to spend three valuable years in the Middle East, or Pakistan or Nepal. Phone Interserve on 071–735 8227 or write to 325 Kennington Road, London SE11 4QH. Of course, denominational societies have their own programmes. Operation Mobilisation presents young people with a challenge to serve Christ through short-term openings in the UK, Europe and on their ships

around the world. They can be contacted at The Quinta, Weston Rhys, Oswestry, Shropshire SY10 7LT. Phone 0691 773388 for information.
● Are you open to God's call for long-term Christian work overseas?
● 'Tent-making', working overseas in your own profession and at the same time serving Christ, is a calling of immense importance. It provides openings in countries otherwise closed to professional missionaries. Information is available from Interserve.

God calls us in many different ways to a whole range of activities. He's looking for people who will respond with commitment; people who are faithful like Timothy.

COMMITTED TO PEOPLE

A commitment which binds us totally to God and his word, and which responds to his call will inevitably involve us with people. Wherever he went Paul gave himself to people – there was nothing half-hearted about it. In Thessalonica the intensity of his love for people comes through powerfully: he's their mother and father in Christ – all rolled into one! We've seen how it worked out in chapter 2, verses 7,8,11,12. People mattered to him, and when he had to leave Thessalonica in a hurry, the parting tore him apart. He refers to it in chapter 2, verse 17: '. . . when we were torn away from you . . . out of our intense longing we made every effort to see you.' Those words 'torn away' reflect a Greek word which literally translated means 'orphaned'. Paul actually felt bereaved when he was torn away from them. He felt as if he had lost children whom God had given him. That was his level of commitment, and he tried again and again to get back to them, without success. So he sent Timothy. His commitment to them was further underlined by the fact that while he was still in Thessalonica, he worked at his trade, tent-making, to avoid being a financial burden. He wanted to help in every way he could, even giving up legitimate demands that he might have made. See how he puts it in chapter 2, verses 7 and 9:

> 'As apostles of Christ we could have been a burden
> to you, but we were gentle among you, like a
> mother . . . Surely you remember, brothers, our toil
> and hardship; we worked night and day in order
> not to be a burden to anyone while we preached the
> gospel of God to you.'

It was all aimed at promoting growth in those to whom he had been sent. He was committed to helping people grow in Christ.

The depth of that commitment is seen in Paul's response when Timothy finally met up with him in Corinth and told him how the Thessalonian Christians were getting on. We read about it in chapter 3, verses 6–8:

> ' . . . Timothy has just now come to us from you and
> has brought good news about your faith and love.
> He has told us that you always have pleasant
> memories of us and that you long to see us, just as
> we also long to see you. Therefore, brothers, in all
> our distress and persecution we were encouraged
> about you because of your faith. For now we really
> live, since you are standing firm in the Lord.'

It seems as if Paul's life was almost falling apart, until he was assured that those Thessalonian Christians whom he loved so deeply were going on, being strengthened, growing in the Lord Jesus Christ. When he discovers that all is well, there can only be one response: 'Now we really live.' That was commitment!

Our commitment, too, is going to be expressed in our involvement with the people around us.

- It may be in the local church, working in a Sunday School class, or in outreach to children.
- Many churches get their members involved in visiting programmes. Have you an opportunity of visiting those who are unwell, elderly; meeting a variety of needs? It's often possible, too, to visit as part of an outreach programme.
- If you have your own home or a room, how about inviting people round for a meal or an evening? Show friendship.
- What about the poor and forgotten people? Local social workers or the Salvation Army may be able to help you get involved.
- Should you develop counselling skills? Scripture Union offers a course in basic counselling skills and a distance learning pack is available for group use. Contact The Training Unit, Scripture Union, 26–30 Heathcoat Street, Nottingham NG1 3AA.

In whatever way we get involved with people around us, our motivation should be the same – God's love and care for those in need. As we've seen several times in 1 Thessalonians 3, Paul refers to love which is intended to grow. This growing love and our commitment are inextricably linked. Chapter 3, verse 12 reads: 'May the Lord make your love increase and overflow for each

other and for everyone else, just as ours does for you.'
And on into the next chapter, verses 9 and 10: '. . . you
yourselves have been taught by God to love each
other . . . Yet we urge you, brothers, to do so more and
more.' So commitment deepens. When it's expressed in
acts of love, it will draw us close to those around us.
We'll discover that there are people with worries, people
with problems, people with grief who need us desperately.

Paul was no stranger to such situations. Chapter
4, verses 13–18 describes his response to a grieving
community. Joy had turned suddenly to anguish when
some in the church died. Unanswered questions plagued
the Christians. Where were their loved one's now? What
would happen when Jesus came back? Would their dead
friends somehow miss out on his coming? Would they
never meet again? Their grief threatened to take on a
'no-hope' conviction – like the pagans around them for
whom death was the inescapable end.

The apostle's response is equal to their agony. He
can't be with them, but he can write: Paul's extracts
the sting from their grief with the assurance that all is
well; they're with Jesus and – amazingly – they'll come
back with him! Paul did what he could: his commitment
had in no way ended when he had left their city limits.
As he had done when he was with them, so now, he
gave his time; a letter prayerfully, lovingly and painstak-
ingly put together.

Giving time to people is tremendously important;
understanding their problems, and their needs. It may
be a letter, a telephone call, or best of all a visit, taking
time to touch, to hold, perhaps to weep, to comfort and
reassure, to pray and take practical action.

Do you recall how Hidayat got up early in the

morning and went out to a sweeper colony? That wasn't a one-off visit. He went again and again, entering into their problems, their difficulties, their heartaches. And hours of work sometimes brought solutions.

Jenny lost her husband tragically in a car accident. She hadn't been married long. There were no children. Jenny was totally shattered. At that time of deep need God was able to work through various members in her local church, but supremely through one friend, who would get alongside her to listen and to talk. Sharing a meal, gradually taking her out to various activities in the church, keeping her involved with what was going on, helping her to grieve, helping her to share – it all helped. Yet it all took a great deal of time. That time was a measure of the care and commitment which God placed in her friend's heart.

Opportunities to express our commitment to people are almost overwhelming, but they are there to be grasped. The list seems endless: people with needs – in broken homes, one-parent families, suffering abuse, experiencing separation and divorce, depression, anxiety, insecurity, stress, loneliness, unemployment, redundancy, victims of prejudice, racism, exploitation, alcoholism . . . They are right there in our churches with many more outside.

Commitment to people is demanding – time-consuming, energy-sapping, emotionally and spiritually draining. But the rewards can be immense, as in many instances healing, stability and progress are experienced. Yet commitment cannot always be seen to succeed. Even so the indispensable demand is for our loving and caring commitment. Paul was a good example; the ultimate model is Jesus.

COMMITTED TO MY LOCAL CHURCH

In our local fellowship the focus of commitment is sharpened. Take a look at chapter 5, verses 12–15, where Paul spells out the kind of commitment that he's looking for:

> 'Now we ask you, brothers, to respect those who
> work hard among you, who are over you in the
> Lord and who admonish you. Hold them in the
> highest regard in love because of their work. Live
> in peace with each other. And we urge you, brothers,
> warn those who are idle, encourage the timid, help
> the weak, be patient with everyone. Make sure that
> nobody pays back wrong for wrong, but always try
> to be kind to each other and to everyone else.'

Paul speaks about different expressions of commitment here. We've already thought in chapter 3 about loving our leaders; it might be good to glance over those pages again, and reaffirm our commitment to them.

Now let's think about our commitment to one another within the fellowship. Look at the imperatives: they're not easy to hold together – *'live in peace with each other . . . warn . . . encourage . . . help . . . be patient.'* And if that's not enough, *don't be vindictive* and *always try to be kind.*

● Look at your church membership list, or if that's too large, at your house group list. Who do you feel needs warning about laziness – do you?! How are they lazy? Now – and here's the crunch question – how can you tackle that laziness, while maintaining a relationship of peace with them? That's not easy. When you've finished, is it more likely to be war than peace?! And if

Paul has in mind the Hebrew concept of peace – well being, wholeness, healing – how is your warning going to contribute to that? Of course, it's not our main calling in the life of the church to go around 'putting everyone right'. We wouldn't be very popular with the leadership if we took that on as our sole role. The challenge, perhaps, is to discover the right method of rebuke. Personal example might help, or an invitation to work alongside someone, or yourself, on a particular project. All the time motivated by a genuine love and understanding. A hefty injection of prayer will help, too. And Paul adds a note about being patient – 'patient with *everyone*'.

● Think about the others around you; the timid and the weak. In what practical ways can you encourage and help?

● Paul knew how common these needs and experiences are, and he raises the subject frequently in his letters. Look up, for example, Ephesians 4:25–32 and Colossians 3:12–17, where similar ideas and needs surface, along with more suggestions for dealing with them.

We come back to 1 Thessalonians 5. Paul's instructions for life and relationships in the fellowship didn't end with verse 15. We're to build on the relationships we've looked at with the characteristics of verses 16–22:

> 'Be joyful always; pray continually; give thanks in all circumstances, for this is God's will for you in Christ Jesus.
>
> Do not put out the Spirit's fire; do not treat prophecies with contempt. Test everything. Hold on to the good. Avoid every kind of evil.'

81

Our commitment to the church can be fuelled with the Spirit's fire. That's good to know – we'll need it.

COMMITTED TO A SPECIFIC LIFESTYLE

Outside the local church, we want our colleagues, families and friends to recognise our commitment. That, frequently, has a great deal to do with our lifestyle, which should be upright and honest, true to Jesus Christ. Paul reminds the Thessalonian Christians of this in chapter 5, verses 4–11. He knows that we live in a dark world, a world in rebellion against God, a world disfigured by abuse, crime, sin. So he writes:

> 'But you, brothers, are not in darkness so that this day should surprise you like a thief. You are all sons of the light and sons of the day. We do not belong to the night or to the darkness. So then, let us not be like others, who are asleep, but let us be alert and self-controlled. For those who sleep, sleep at night, and those who get drunk, get drunk at night. But since we belong to the day, let us be self-controlled, putting on faith and love as a breastplate, and the hope of salvation as a helmet. For God did not appoint us to suffer wrath but to receive salvation through our Lord Jesus Christ. He died for us so that, whether we are awake or asleep, we may live together with him. Therefore encourage one another and build each other up, just as in fact you are doing.'

We live in a dark world, but that's a backcloth which heightens a contrast. We are sons and daughters of the light. The Lord Jesus, the light of the world, has enlightened our lives; he is a light that has revolution-ised our lifestyle. So, we're to be distinct from the dark world in which we live; not asleep but awake, alert, self-controlled. That adds up to discipline: learning not to budge under pressure, not to give in to what is evil.

Frank, a Christian salesman, had a responsible job – selling printing equipment over a large part of Africa. The contracts were immense, running into millions. As he went from country to country, seeking to interest governments and large private corporations, he was confronted again and again with one major problem – bribery. Customers wanted their palms greased before they would place an order. They made him attractive offers to benefit from their corruption. Frank was in a dilemma. He needed the orders, but how, as a Christian, could he cope with corrupt pressures? There it was: no concessions, no contracts. Frank did a lot of thinking, and finally the decision was made: lucrative as the job was, he had to quit. He would look for other employ-ment where his moral standing would not be corrupted and destroyed.

That's the choice Christians have to make when they are committed to living with integrity and honesty. And, at a time when work is not always easy to get, the temptations are great. Commitment calls for an attitude of no compromise.

● Are there aspects of your job which compromise your commitment to a Christian lifestyle?

In a dark world, we're involved in warfare – warfare with evil. Paul underlines this in verse 8 of the passage, where he says:

'. . . let us be self-controlled, putting on faith and

> love as a breastplate, and the hope of salvation as
> a helmet.'

In Ephesians chapter 6 the apostle elaborates this idea of the Christian's armour, but the three factors which he mentions here to the Thessalonians are of crucial importance in our conflict with corruption of any kind. Here we have faith, love and hope strengthening us as we fight against the evil one. That's what we need: faith that will not yield under pressure; love that cares more about people than personal profit; hope that keeps salvation before our eyes all the time, helping us to get our objectives right.

It won't be easy. There are other contrary – and in many ways enticing – lifestyles all around us. Undoubtedly, we need the teaching of God's word to guide our attitudes and actions, but along with that we also need friends, with whom we can talk issues through and who can encourage us to make the right decisions – and to stick with them. That was the situation in Thessalonica. Christians there needed help to stand firm. So Paul writes in verse 11:

> 'Therefore encourage one another and build each
> other up, just as in fact you are doing.'

Our commitment to a Christian lifestyle is certainly going to come under pressure.

● Make sure that you have friends who will stand by you and be an example. They may well need your support, too.

COMMITTED TO PRAY

Finally, Paul highlights a commitment to prayer. We shall be dealing with the subject separately, but here perhaps we should ask ourselves just one question – how committed are we to prayer?

Someone says, 'Please pray for me.' We respond immediately, genuinely, but almost without thinking, 'Yes, of course I will.' And, then we promptly go and forget all about it. It was a request that Paul himself made in chapter 5, verse 25: 'Brothers, pray for us.' I wonder how many of those Thessalonians really took that request seriously. Only recently in a house group, Jim, one of the members, rang up. It was late. He couldn't make it, he explained, because he had been to the dentist to have a wisdom tooth out, and his jaw was still painful.

'Sorry, I can't come,' he went on. 'Please pray for me. It's hurting quite badly.'

'Of course we will. Don't worry. We'll add it to the other items at the end of the meeting.'

And the reply came back, 'Well, please do remember.' Jim knew that enthusiastic responses aren't always acted on. He was right. At the end of the meeting we forgot.

It may be something far more serious than a passing toothache, though that can be urgent. But whatever the need – great or small – we're to be people who can be relied on, friends committed to pray for each other.

There are various methods which can help us to be faithful:

• There is the Prayer Triplet scheme. The Evangelical Alliance produce small Prayer Triplet booklets which are designed for use by three people who get together to pray and intercede. Phone 071–582 0228.

● You may prefer to make your own note-book, putting requests in various columns, and keeping a column, too, for answers.

● Perhaps you receive prayer letters and other pieces of information. Why not put them in a loose-leaf file, and work through them regularly? That's what we now do at home. We have friends all around the world, who write to us, sharing information for praise and prayer. It's all too easy just to read them, put them on one side, and forget about them. By putting them into a file, categorising them under countries, we can work our way through week by week.

● One spin-off is that you get to know your friends far more intimately as their news and requests are regularly prayed for. But, far more important, you have the privilege of standing alongside them in their experiences, looking to God to react to their needs. That's an added stimulus to keep in touch, looking for the evidence of God hearing and answering prayers.

Being committed, then, affects every aspect of life, and means commitment to God, his word and our calling. It ties us strongly to people and to our local church. It stimulates us to examine our lifestyle, and carries us forward to consistent prayer for one another. It's a growing experience. Check up on your growth!

5

GROW IN
HOLINESS

Holiness is a way of living that means being 'set apart for God'. It's an expression of our commitment to him, a determination to please him by the way we live. That's how Paul put it in 1 Thessalonians 4:1:

> 'Finally brothers, we instructed you how to live in order to please God, as in fact you are living.'

So how do I please God?

It was a typical warm, bustling afternoon in the centre of Kathmandu, capital of Nepal, the world's only Hindu kingdom. Standing outside one of the city's many ornate temples was an Indian sadhu. His hair was long and matted, as was his beard. Round his neck were several necklaces, his robes were saffron, his forehead whitened with ash, and in its centre, a scarlet dot. His right hand held a staff, almost like a crook, with little bells attached, hanging from the heads of three carved cobras. We talked together about his search for holiness and peace. This holy man had travelled far – from the south of India near Cape Comorin, up through the holy city of Madurai, with its vast array of temples; on to Varanasi on the mighty Ganges to drink its holy, sin-cleansing water. Now his search for holiness had brought him far to the north – to Kathmandu.

'Sadhuji,' I asked him, 'have you found what you are looking for?' He replied with a shake of his head: 'No, I'm still looking.'

WHAT IS HOLINESS?

Where do you find holiness? I'm sure I saw it in a small clinic, many hundreds of miles to the south, in Pakistan. Alison was a nurse and midwife, and she had been up for most of the night. Now with a quickly snatched breakfast and a wash, she had gone to the clinic. The courtyard was full with women, ante-natal, post-natal cases, some with tuberculosis, others with little children, similarly ill. The hours of the morning passed slowly, and the crowd didn't seem to diminish. One after another, they were examined, treated, advised – a kind word, a touch on the head of a little child, a prescription made out, tablets supplied, an injection given. She seemed tired, but she still kept going. She even found time to talk to some of the patients about their families, things that concerned them. And that night, too, I guessed she might well be called out to another delivery.

What is holiness? What do you think of when the word is mentioned? Stained glass windows, halos round the heads of the church's saints, hands folded in prayer and devotion, monks or nuns set apart in cells to pray? Church history records them: men and women who sought to give their lives to God in a special way. Some were famous, many unknown, Some were extraordinary, like Simon Stylites, who in his quest for holiness spent the last years of his life sitting on top of a pole, isolated. Perhaps that was his idea of being separated for God.

But if I take special orders and vows, does it make me holy? If I take the vow of silence, there's no unholy language, but what of my thoughts? If I take a vow of poverty, I have no physical riches, but what happens to the greed in my heart? Or if I take a vow of celibacy, I may escape sexual immorality, but what of lust that can hide deep within? That perhaps points us to the real seat of holiness, because it starts with a radical change deep inside us. With it comes the birth of new desires; to be done with sin, to love good. And then it's expressed outwardly, as I turn my back on evil, going after what is truly good.

What does the word mean?
What, however, does the word itself mean? Well, that's quite simple. It means 'to be set apart'. And for a Christian it means to be dedicated, or to dedicate, consecrate, sanctify. So I consecrate myself to God. That involves becoming morally like him. Peter refers to this when he writes: '. . . just as he who called you is holy, so be holy in all you do; for it is written: "Be holy, because I am holy" ' (1 Peter 1:15,16). That's an attitude and a condition that reminds us of Jesus. Peter goes on:

> 'To this you were called, because Christ suffered for you, leaving you an example, that you should follow in his steps. "He committed no sin, and no deceit was found in his mouth." When they hurled their insults at him, he did not retaliate; when he suffered he made no threats.' *1 Peter 2:21–23*

Jesus was certainly set apart for God. And if we're Christians, that's the route we'll be wanting to follow, as we try to discover how we can be holy.

GOD MAKES THE FIRST MOVE

We quickly discover that it's God who makes the first move; Father, Son and Holy Spirit, working together, enabling each of us gradually to become like him – set apart for him. God was at work in Thessalonica from the very beginning. We've already seen how in chapter 1, verse 4 Paul writes: 'Brothers loved by God, we know that he has chosen you.' He had chosen them to become like his Son the Lord Jesus Christ. This change began when, as Paul shared God's word with them, the Holy Spirit worked in their hearts bringing deep conviction, both of sin and also of his power to change them into holy people (v 5). That's how God works, and continues to work, with the constant aim of making our lives holy. Paul underlines this later in his letter in chapter 4, verse 7 when he writes:

> 'For God did not call us to be impure, but to live a holy life.'

God's call, his purpose for us and the help he offers through his Holy Spirit are there; it's plain and clear. But, unfortunately, we can ignore or reject it. Paul had to go on to remind the Thessalonians in chapter 5, verse 19 of just that possibility: 'Do not put out the Spirit's fire.' The Good News Bible and the Revised Standard Version use similar words that reinforce the idea: 'Do not restrain the Holy Spirit' . . . 'Do not quench the

Holy Spirit.' That's possible. We can restrain, quench, put out the Holy Spirit's purifying fire, as Christians turning our backs on holy living. It may be for a moment, an evening, a day. And we discover that days can lengthen into weeks, weeks into months . . . into years. But the amazing thing is that God perseveres with us. He doesn't give up, and Paul banks on it, as his final prayer in chapter 5, verses 23, 24 makes clear,

> 'May God himself, the God of peace, sanctify you [make you holy] through and through. May your whole spirit, soul and body be kept blameless at the coming of our Lord Jesus Christ. The one who calls you is faithful and he will do it.'

That's the persevering God. He's here to help right now.

WE CAN HELP EACH OTHER

God through his Holy Spirit is near to help, and that's tremendously encouraging. But perhaps, like me, you also find that a visible help is often what we need – a real, live, flesh-and-blood example of everyday, personal holiness. Paul and his friends were just that kind of example. He writes in chapter 2, verse 10; 'You are witnesses, and so is God, of how holy, righteous and blameless we were among you who believed.' Some example! But don't let the idea of an apostolic super-saint-status mask the issue. Paul and his colleagues were real – sometimes failing – Christians; but nevertheless, Christians who could be an encouragement to those who watched them.

Notice those three words which are inter-related:

'holy, righteous and blameless.' Holy people are those, as we've already seen, who are 'set apart for God'. Now 'righteous' and 'blameless' come alongside to show what everyday holiness is going to involve. So the holy person is 'righteous'; someone who has an upright character, a man or woman of integrity. He refuses to get involved in crooked thinking, speech or action. Her promises can be trusted. Jesus spoke about that kind of person in Matthew chapter 5, verse 16: 'Let your light shine before men, that they may see your good deeds and praise your Father in heaven.'

The 'blameless' life provides another slant on holiness. Paul is not claiming a sinless perfection – everyone has one-off failures. But he is asserting that there are no skeletons in the cupboard. Have you heard someone say, 'He's OK, but . . .' and go on to specify a character deficiency, a recurring weakness? The 'blameless' life is open to scrutiny, given over to God.

- Is there a way in which you could be more 'righteous' or 'blameless' in your work place?
- Look out for friends with that quality, for when we see their example being lived out in front of us, we'll be encouraged and helped to take on board holiness as it really is in practical terms.
- We can also help one another to be holy through prayer. Paul illustrates this in chapter 3, verse 13, where he himself prays for the Thessalonian Christians;

> 'May he strengthen your hearts so that you will be blameless and holy in the presence of our God and Father when our Lord Jesus comes with all his holy ones.'

WHAT SHOULD I CONCENTRATE ON?

There is a general answer that can be given immediately. Concentrate on every aspect of life! Nothing is excluded. That's the point of Paul's prayer in chapter 5, verse 23 where he says:

> May God himself, the God of peace, sanctify you [make you holy] *through and through*.'

Or as the Good News Bible puts it:

> 'May the God who gives us peace make you holy *in every way* and keep your *whole being* – spirit, soul and body . . .'.

● Every part of me is to be made holy, in every situation, in every experience.

AVOID IMMORALITY

However, the apostle doesn't leave them with generalisations. There were specific areas in their lives which were under threat. No doubt the needs of individual Thessalonians varied, just as our needs vary. However, for them and for us there was a major, and potentially devastating, danger: sexual immorality.

Today we can't over-estimate this menace, with the tragedies which follow in its wake. In Paul's day the Greek cities were infamous and the Roman world no better. So Paul tackles head-on this assault on holiness – on the morality of God's people. See how he puts it in chapter 4, verses 1–8:

> 'Finally brothers, we instructed you how to live in

order to please God, as in fact you are living. Now we ask you and urge you in the Lord Jesus to do this more and more. You know what instructions we gave you by the authority of the Lord Jesus.

It is God's will that you should be holy; that you should avoid sexual immorality; that each of you should learn to control his own body in a way that is holy and honourable, not in passionate lust like the heathen, who do not know God; and that in this matter no one should wrong his brother or take advantage of him. The Lord will punish men for all such sins, as we have already told you and warned you. For God did not call us to be impure, but to live a holy life. Therefore he who rejects this instruction does not reject man but God, who gives you his Holy Spirit.'

The Thessalonian Christians hadn't fallen into the immorality trap, but Paul needed to warn them. To be forewarned is vitally important, for there was always the possibility that some of them might be engulfed. So he underlines the danger: 'we have already told you and warned you.' While sexual immorality is a problem for a lot of people, it may not be a temptation which as yet has hit you with overwhelming force. But sooner or later that temptation may well become real. So it's necessary to warn.

It's important, too, to be specific. Paul is just that. He doesn't mince his words, but goes on to stress that he had given them 'instructions . . . by the authority of the Lord Jesus'. And the instructions were clear: 'It is God's will that you should be holy; that you should avoid sexual immorality.'

The Bible's teaching on sexual morality is under

attack; living the kind of life that the word of God sets out for us is not popular. The mass media, with its access to us through popular magazines, radio and television, bombard us with concepts that are immoral. All this makes an appeal to our own human sinfulness, our selfishness and greed, which respond to the kind of programmes that the media present to us. Paul defines this in verse 5 as, 'passionate lust', and it's there potentially, if not actively, in each of us.

Secular counselling seeks to deal with the problem and gives much helpful advice. Knowing what makes us tick, they will advise the use of a condom, and stress the importance of having a regular partner. But, rarely, if ever, will abstinence be suggested as a realistic option. The majority regard it as an impossibility.

Two years ago we were skiing in the shadow of the Eiger, at Kleine Scheidegg in Switzerland. At lunchtime, as we sat in the snow near the railway station, a group of young people came along wearing T-shirts, which carried the slogan: 'Beat AIDS'. Round they went, handing out free condoms, and emphasising the need to use them when we went to bed that night. They were staggered to hear from several single people in the group, that they didn't plan to use condoms that night, but that as Christians we believed that sex outside marriage wasn't on. It was something we could wait for until God brought us into a marriage relationship.

The world doesn't think that way, and yet the effects of sexual immorality are increasingly devastating. We see how it leads to family breakdown, divorce or separation. Or if a marriage holds together, a niggling distrust of one's partner. Again, sexual immorality can result in abortion, as the high incidence of this in our own society testifies. It's frequently seen, too, in the many instances of single parenthood. Then there are sexually transmitted diseases: syphilis, gonorrhoea; the increasing possibility of being HIV positive or having AIDS. The world faces a massive disaster as millions of people become infected with this, as yet, incurable condition. And for many, too, who have none of these symptoms, there is a deep sense of guilt which refuses to go away.

So what does Paul say? What is the Bible's solution? It's set out clearly in chapter 4, verse 3: 'Avoid sexual immorality.' And that's the consistent teaching of the word of God. We find four plain words in 1 Corinthians chapter 6, verse 18: 'Flee from sexual immorality.'

Returning to the Thessalonian situation, Paul spells out four important issues in verses 4–8.

• *Control your body*: '. . . each of you should learn to control his own body in a way that is holy and honourable' (v 4). There are two possible translations of these words: either as above, or as in the NIV margin: '. . . learn to live with his own wife in a way that is holy . . .' Both translations are valid, and both are important. It's essential to master our bodies – keeping ourselves holy, and equally important to have a right view of marriage, honouring its holiness.

• *Lust is not Christian*: we're to control our own bodies 'in a way that is holy and honourable, *not in passionate lust like the heathen.*'

• *Other people suffer*: '. . . in this matter no one should wrong his brother' (v 6). To have sex with a married woman who is not one's wife is to sin against her husband. Sin doesn't end there, for we have to reckon with God.

• *God punishes sin*: 'The Lord will punish for all such sins' (v 6). There's a stark finality here when we abandon God's call to holiness: '. . . he who rejects this instruction does not reject man but God . . .' (v 8).

WHAT ABOUT FORGIVENESS?

Is there then no forgiveness? That was the question which worried Dr Alex. As a student he had become friendly with a girl in the same college, and they started to sleep together. This went on for about a year. Then, convicted that what they were doing was wrong, they had broken up.

'Can God really forgive me?' he asked. 'I knew it was wrong, but for a whole year . . .' Alex was convinced that he was a write-off: living a truly Christian life was beyond his reach.

The wonderful thing is, of course, that God does forgive, for when the Lord Jesus grants us forgiveness, it's total and complete. Sin calls for repentance and confession, but the forgiveness is there. We turned to 1 Corinthians 6:9–11.

> 'Do you not know that the wicked will not inherit the kingdom of God? Do not be deceived: Neither the sexually immoral nor idolaters nor adulterers nor male prostitutes nor homosexual offenders nor thieves nor the greedy nor drunkards nor slanderers nor swindlers will inherit the kingdom of God. And that is what some of you were. But you were washed, you were sanctified, you were justified in the name of the Lord Jesus Christ and by the Spirit of our God.'

It was there that Alex found complete release. Although he had done what was wrong, he was sorry. The Lord Jesus had washed him, washed him clean, even though at that moment he could hardly realise it. Then it dawned with all its wonder. He was actually clean – holy in God's sight. And he discovered a joy that he hadn't known for years. God punishes, but God also forgives – totally.

Janet was a teacher from one of the south London boroughs who had a slightly different problem. Her comment was, 'I know I'm forgiven, but I feel that I can never be really holy.' She explained how she had gone to bed with her boyfriend. She knew it was wrong, but had done it all the same. Afterwards, truly sorry, she had asked for forgiveness, and was convinced that God had forgiven her.

'But I don't feel that I can ever be really holy,' she insisted. It was as if some indelible mark scarred her personality, cutting her off from the possibility of ever really being used by God.

'I feel as I've been put on one side,' Janet concluded, 'that I'm spoilt – not good enough for God to use.'

It was that verse in 1 Corinthians chapter 6 that finally cleared the air, enabling her to see that God had put everything right: 'You were washed, you were sanctified, you were justified in the name of the Lord Jesus Christ and by the Spirit of our God.' She knew now that she could go on and really be holy, set apart for God to do whatever he wanted.

Janet had found it helpful to talk over the problem with someone who cared, and that's always a good idea.

Moral living, then, is *a way of pleasing God*. That's

how Paul puts it in 1 Thessalonians 4:1. He goes on to make it clear in verse 8 that moral living is also *a command from God*. Yet pressures pile up on us, and sometimes we're tempted to feel that holiness is going to be beyond us. If so, there's a word of strong encouragement in verse 8. We're assured that God gives us his Spirit. Satan may tempt us to reject God's call to sexual morality and holiness, but there, all the time within us, is God's Holy Spirit.

There's the help, there's the strength. He's the Spirit who is holy in himself and who is committed to making us holy. In this area of sexual morality, as in every other area of life, he's one who's called alongside to help. He'll help us to grow in holiness, as daily we hand over our lives to him.

6
GROW AS
EXAMPLES

We all need good examples; people who make an impact on us. They can be any age – elderly, or teenage. They can be children for that matter; boys and girls can be tremendous examples in their simplicity of faith. They really trust God to do things. Among young people there can be outstanding examples of commitment and courage; their willingness to go to any length to serve the Lord Jesus Christ. And, of course, accumulated experience over many years often enables older folk to become valuable models. In most people's experience there will be one or two individuals whose lives have been influential.

I recall the example of Dr John Laird. He was General Secretary of Scripture Union for many years, and also an elder in my own local church. He became a spiritual father. Qualities I appreciated, and which proved good examples for me, were his transparent goodness and kindness. He was committed to the truth; you could rely on his word. He was trustworthy. There was an approachable quality about him; a ready smile, and a warm welcome. His friendship was treasured, and he stuck by those who needed him. He was interested, too, in all the major and minor details of one's life, with their pressures and joys. John Laird was a wise man, and his sound, practical advice was often sought. A strong sense of humour kept him attractively human. As a leader, his qualities were outstanding, as he guided Scripture Union's work not only in the UK but also was influential in developing it worldwide. Dr Laird's was a moulding influence extending over many years. Such people are invaluable: their example to be treasured.

Other examples stand out because they make their impact on us at a critical point in our experience: a time, perhaps, when we need to change direction or make important decisions. They're important, too.

Deryck Thompson had a room next to mine on the Air Force station at Palam outside Delhi in India. I had just been brought back to the Lord Jesus Christ, and I needed to get down to Bible study, to be firmly established as a Christian. There Deryck proved to be a tremendous help. He was an electrical officer on our station, carrying considerable responsibility, but there were priorities in his life which became examples to the rest of us. He made Bible study – personal Bible study – a major priority. That equipped him to teach, and the teaching he gave to that small Christian group on the Air Force station was valued. He was an example, too, in sharing his faith. Other officers in the mess and in various parts of the station where he worked, knew where he stood and what he believed. He was a man of integrity; his word was trustworthy. I found that a tremendous help as I started to grow as a Christian, and began to seek God's will for my life in the future.

But behind all that, I had known the example of

good parents, who laid a foundation of church attendance, Bible reading, and basic training in Christian living. I had thrown so much of that overboard, but there it was as a base, a good example to which I could return.

And, of course, spanning so many of those years is the example of a good wife; the kindness, the unselfishness, the faithfulness that I've seen consistently. My wife, Joanne, has proved an example worth following.

GOOD EXAMPLES ARE IMPORTANT

So there will be different examples at different times in our lives, as different needs confront us, and as we gradually develop. Those good examples are people God can use.

Two such people we find in Thessalonica: Paul and Timothy. They had a tremendous relationship between them, and Paul had been an indispensable example to Timothy while he grew as a young Christian. Subsequently, Paul was able to send Timothy off on a variety of assignments, knowing that his example would stand Timothy in good stead. This comes across clearly when he writes to Timothy in his second letter:

> 'You then, my son, be strong in the grace that is in Christ Jesus. And the things you have heard me say in the presence of many witnesses entrust to reliable men who will also be qualified to teach others.'
>
> *2 Timothy 2:1, 2*

Paul had been an example of good teaching to Timothy, which, he in turn was now able to pass on. Similarly, in Thessalonica Paul saw himself as an example to be copied. In chapter 1, verse 6 Paul reminds the believers that: 'You became imitators of us and of the Lord.' He repeats this in his second letter, in chapter 3, verse 7, where he writes: 'For you yourselves know how you ought to follow our example.'

A LEADERSHIP ROLE

So we discover that a major role for any leader is to be an example to those for whom he's responsible. And that will apply to us at whatever level of responsibility we operate.

In contrast – unfortunately – many of us often feel almost forced to say, 'Do as I say, but not as I do.' 'Don't scrutinise too closely the way I actually behave. I know the answers. You just take them on board.' That wasn't the way Paul operated. When he wrote to the Corinthians, he said, '. . . I urge you to imitate me. For this reason I am sending to you Timothy, my son whom I love, who is faithful in the Lord. He will remind you of my way of life in Christ Jesus, which agrees with what I teach everywhere in every church.' (1 Corinthians 4:16, 17).

It wasn't only to the Corinthians; he could write similarly to the Philippians, presenting himself as a personal example to them: 'Whatever you have learned or received or heard from me, or seen in me – put it into practice. And the God of peace will be with you' (Philippians 4:9).

The general principle emerges in Hebrews, where the writer states: 'Remember your leaders, who spoke the word of God to you. Consider the outcome of their way of life and imitate their faith' (Hebrews 13:7).

The whole of Scripture combines to emphasise this point, that leaders are to be copied; they are to be men and women of stature, good examples.

But whether leaders are good examples or bad ones, they are going to be copied. There's Diotrephes who is mentioned in John's third letter, verses 9, 10 – a bad example. He tried consistently to dominate the church, and with equal consistency was a malicious gossip. Any who objected he threw out of the church! Bearing Diotrephes' lifestyle in mind, John comments, '. . . do not imitate what is evil but what is good.' In contrast, Paul comes through as a model who can be confidently followed. In fact, he uses almost those exact words when he writes to the Thessalonians in his second letter, referring to his aim, together with Silas and Timothy, '. . . to make ourselves a model for you to follow' (2 Thessalonians 3:9).

That's how some of those examples in my own Christian life have appeared to me. Deryck Thompson, as part of his responsibilities at the Air Force station, in Palam, India, would have regular meetings with the station commander along with other officers in charge of various units. The station commander would brief them, question them, hear their reports, comment on needs and activities. One day, he was angered by a certain situation which had developed, and started to swear profusely. Suddenly, he stopped. Looking at Deryck Thompson, whom he knew as a committed Christian, he said, 'I'm sorry, Thompson, I forgot you were here.' Deryck had become an example, of whom even the station commander was conscious.

• Good examples make their mark. If you have any kind of leadership role, at work, home or church what mark are you aiming for? Good examples influence those around them, whether it's at work, at home, in the church or house group, youth sector or Christian Union.

• Take time to think through the needs of your own particular church group, identifying areas where these examples are needed: examples of a consistent Christian lifestyle – integrity, patience, kindness, goodness, faithfulness, gentleness, self-control, compassion, humility, forgiveness, holiness, love, reliability . . . Fill out the details, setting the qualities required into the context of real-life situations.

THE INFALLIBLE EXAMPLE

You may be conscious of ways in which the Lord could use you as an effective example; conscious too, perhaps of deficiency or failure. But there is one infallible example, and that is Jesus himself.

Significantly, Paul doesn't set himself up as a sole example. When he writes to the Thessalonians he reminds them that; 'You became imitators of us *and of the Lord*' (1 Thessalonians 1:6). To the Corinthians he writes, 'Follow my example, *as I follow the example of Christ*' (1 Corinthians 11:1). And to the Ephesians, '*Be imitators of God* . . . as dearly loved children' (Ephesians 5:1).

Paul, then, points us to God and to the Lord Jesus whom he sought to follow and imitate. That's encouraging, for whatever our measure of success or failure as examples, we can point others to Jesus Christ as the ultimate and complete model.

● Look again at the list of qualities of Christian character in the previous section. Put them alongside incidents in the life of Jesus. Does his example stand up untarnished?

● Point people to Jesus. But we must be careful not to use him as a means for getting ourselves off the hook. We still have a responsibility to walk in the steps of Christ. Those around us need to see Jesus working in us and through us.

So God works in a two-fold way. First, he sets his own character before us in Jesus and calls us to follow and imitate him. Second, he encourages us to look at Christlike people, and to find there an incentive for Christ-centred living.

Whether we're leaders or followers – or a bit of both – it's important to keep our eyes open for good examples. We'll find them in the church, and in our wider Christian contacts. They may be leaders of our local fellowship; elders, deacons or ministers; they could be youth leaders or Sunday School teachers or in the close circle of our own friends. Wherever we find them, value them highly!

But just as good examples are needed, so are good imitators. In this, too, we can be like those Thessalonian Christians. Look again at chapter 1, verse 6, and this time place the emphasis on the first half of the sentence: '*You became imitators of us* and of the Lord.' They had fastened on to the good qualities that came through in Paul and Timothy's lives, and they made them a model for their own conduct.

EXAMPLES IN HANDLING OPPOSITION

It's worth looking at the particular areas in which the Thessalonians followed Paul's example. They may well be important areas for us too. They soon discovered how Paul handled opposition and suffering. And they were quick learners! That takes us once more to chapter 1, verse 6, where Paul says of them:

> 'You became imitators of us and of the Lord; in spite of severe suffering, you welcomed the message with the joy given by the Holy Spirit.'

Paul's attitude to opposition had become infectious. He wasn't cowed or beaten down by it. Their reaction had corresponded to his. They knew perfectly well how he had reacted in Philippi; he had kept on sharing the good news about Jesus. Paul reminds them of that experience:

> 'We had previously suffered and been insulted in Philippi, as you know, but with the help of our God we dared to tell you his gospel in spite of strong opposition.'   1 Thessalonians 2:2

Similarly, faced with opposition, the Thessalonians weren't halted in their tracks. Like Paul, they took it head on, and went out to share God's message with others. Chapter 1, verse 8 reminds us of it:

> 'The Lord's message rang out from you not only in Macedonia and Achaia – your faith in God has become known everywhere.'

They were good models. And we find in chapter 2, verse 14 that they were part of a tremendous reaction which characterised the whole early church, for they were also imitating the Judean churches in their response to opposition. So Paul writes:

> 'For you, brothers, became imitators of God's churches in Judea, which are in Christ Jesus: You suffered from your own countrymen the same things those churches suffered from the Jews . . .'

The reaction of the Judean churches to the intense opposition, which scattered them throughout Palestine, was not to keep quiet, but to spread the good news whenever they found an opportunity. For example, we read in Acts 8:1–8 how Philip – and probably others – went to Samaria. As a result of their coming, the whole city was turned upside down, and God sent a revival! Similarly, despite opposition these Thessalonian Christians had taken God's word far beyond their own city, to the surrounding area of Macedonia and Achaia – a region covering the whole of modern Greece and beyond into southern Bulgaria and the Yugoslav republics. They certainly latched on to their examples!

The inevitable conclusion to draw is that if you see someone standing up to opposition, you'll be encouraged to do so, too. That certainly was their experience as they followed the examples of both Paul and the Judean churches.

That was how Jim reacted. He wasn't a Christian, but the person who worked alongside him in the machine shop at their local factory in Birmingham was. Jim watched him carefully. His lifestyle was different from the others in the factory. So was his language. There were the negative elements: things he didn't do, like swearing, sharing in filthy language and jokes. Lying and dishonesty were out. But there were other things that he did do, things which were attractive. If anybody needed help, he was there to give it. He was kind and understanding. And much to the amusement of most of them in that section of the factory, he used to leave tracts lying around in the wash room. It was one of those tracts that Jim picked up. He took it home and glanced over it, but it made little or no impression.

Then came Christmas Eve. Jim was in the pub, downing his third pint, when, suddenly, he slammed down his tankard, turned on his heel and went out, saying to himself, 'For the last seven years, I've been drinking myself stupid on Christmas Eve, and spending Christmas Day getting over the hangover.'

He went and searched around in his room until he found that crumpled tract, and started to read it again. As he read, the truth dawned, and he asked Jesus to be his Saviour. It wasn't just the tract. It was the total impact on his life of a man who worked alongside him and who was different, in whose life he saw the character of Jesus Christ, and was attracted by it. He had handled the jibes, the ridicule and the opposition that came because of his way of living. They had all made their impact on Jim, and he told us with a smile, 'Now they're watching two of us like hawks!' He was learning to be an example, too.

• As a Christian you will be watched at work. What do you think are the qualities which they need to see in your life in order to be challenged about their own attitudes and lifestyles, and to be attracted to Christ?

EXAMPLES IN LIFESTYLE

But, it's not just in handling opposition that we can become good examples; it's in our general attitude to work and, in fact, our whole lifestyle, as Jim discovered. The Thessalonians had seen this in the apostle Paul. He had worked hard, as he reminds them:

> 'Surely you remember, brothers, our toil and hardship; we worked night and day in order not to be a burden to anyone while we preached the gospel of God to you.'   *1 Thessalonians 2:9*

And he repeats the same idea in his second letter:

> 'For you yourselves know how you ought to follow our example. We were not idle when we were with you, nor did we eat anyone's food without paying for it. On the contrary, we worked night and day, labouring and toiling so that we would not be a burden to any of you. We did this, not because we do not have the right to such help, but in order to make ourselves a model for you to follow.'
> *2 Thessalonians 3:7–9*

It's important to have the right attitude in our daily work situations. Paul makes a specific reference to this in chapter 4, verses 11,12:

> 'Make it your ambition to lead a quiet life, to mind your own business and to work with your hands, just as we told you, so that your daily life may win the respect of outsiders and so that you will not be dependent on anybody.'

Paul was correcting some of the excesses in the Thessalonian church, but the underlying emphasis here is to be industrious and hard-working. Such lives earn respect, and impose no burdens on others. That same attitude still has relevance in a welfare state. The way we live will either attract people to Christ, or put them off.

Frank's a carpenter on a building site. After watching him for some weeks, a young engineer, Roger, wanted to know why Frank was so different from the rest of the crew. Things about him which had caught Roger's attention were quite ordinary but significant: his consistent hard work, no time wasting, his honesty and cheerfulness. And he had sometimes noticed Frank reading his Bible during meal breaks! It wasn't hard for Frank to explain how Jesus made all the difference to his lifestyle, for Roger was already convinced that Frank had something which was worth following up.

● It's good to be that kind of example. Think about your family, friends and colleagues. What conclusions might they be coming to?

EXAMPLES OF CHRISTIAN CHARACTER

It's not just in the way we handle opposition or how we conduct ourselves at work. We can also become valuable examples through the development of our Christian characters. It could be seen in Jim's friend and also in Frank, and it's there regardless of circumstances – whether there's opposition or interest. Indeed, it's that which sparks both of them off. A consistent Christian character becomes a potent example; encouraging other Christians to strive for the same reality, as well as sending a powerful message to those who as yet don't know Jesus.

Christian characters aren't put together overnight. It takes time, along with the whole range of experiences that life throws at us. But the process starts as soon as we come to Christ, and his Holy Spirit begins to cultivate his fruit. Undoubtedly, both Paul and Timothy had been powerful examples to the Thessalonians at this level. Paul's love, gentleness, uprightness, blamelessness and holiness must have made a tremendous impact, challenging and spurring the new Christians on to cultivate the same qualities through the Spirit who had also come to them.

But what about Timothy? Little is said about him in this letter to the Thessalonians, beyond the fact that he 'is our brother and God's fellow-worker' (3:2). A pretty strong statement! But Timothy's younger. Has he really got the calibre of Christian character that the Thessalonians need to see? Paul knows he has. We get an insight into Timothy's character when Paul writes to him personally sometime later at Ephesus:

> 'Don't let anyone look down on you because you are
> young, but set an example for the believers in
> speech, in life, in love, in faith and in purity.'

Paul emphasises five points of importance for Timothy. The first two relate to activity, and tie in with Jim and Frank's experiences. The last three, however, are essential basic ingredients to the building of Christian character.

Timothy may be young but he's had the privilege of working alongside Paul for years, seeing his love, faith and purity being expressed in action. He's learnt from these experiences and grown as a result. It's encouraging also to realise that love, faith and purity are not the products solely of long experience or old age, but of the Holy Spirit who lives in us. So whether in Thessalonica or Ephesus Timothy could be the kind of example the Christians needed to see.

● The 'disciple/teacher' relationship is still something to go for. Look out for men and women in whom you see those Christ-like qualities, and get to know them and seek their friendship. See how they react to difficult situations, challenges, disappointments, opportunities. See how they respond to people; how they work alongside, nurture and encourage them. You may not always agree with everything – no one's perfect! But they can be valuable models.

● In taking stock of the way our Christian characters are developing, it may be helpful to ask ourselves how others – not just our friends – would rate us in the light of these three qualities, love, faith and purity, that Paul expected to find in Timothy, and in the Thessalonian Christians.

● In what ways can Christians turn people off? If you were working along with a Christian who through inconsistency or some other failure was having a negative influence, how would you try to remedy the situation?

IMITATORS BECOME MODELS

Good imitators become good models. Our shape as models will to a large degree be determined by the models we ourselves select to copy . . . Christ? Paul?

Timothy? Our own church leaders? Friends? Select models carefully and with prayer.

The Thessalonians made the grade, and Paul was delighted. So he congratulates them:

> '... you became a model to all the believers in
> Macedonia and Achaia.'   *1 Thessalonians 1:7*

There's no doubt about it; we will have people copying us. They will see our attitudes to opposition, the way we behave at work, the way our characters reflect the personality of Jesus Christ, the way our love is expressed in action. Their faith will grow if our faith is seen to be unshakeable. And as we live pure lives in an impure society, so they will be strengthened and encouraged to take their stand. God is looking for growth.

• So there's another useful question we might ask ourselves: Am I a better example now than I was a year ago? In what areas is there growth? Where has there been failure? Go back to your greatest model. Jesus is only too willing to help when you talk it over with him.

GUIDELINES FOR MODELS

Take a final look at chapter 5, verses 14–24. Paul sets out here some good guidelines for models involved in the business of daily living:

> '... we urge you, brothers, warn those who are idle,
> encourage the timid, help the weak, be patient with
> everyone. Make sure that nobody pays back wrong
> for wrong, but always try to be kind to each other
> and to everyone else.

Be joyful always; pray continually; give thanks in all circumstances, for this is God's will for you in Christ Jesus.

Do not put out the Spirit's fire; do not treat prophecies with contempt. Test everything. Hold on to the good. Avoid every kind of evil.'

● Select just a few instructions – three or four – and aim to put them into action over the coming weeks so that your life will be a better example in your family, in church, and in your workplace.

7

GROW IN
THE SPIRIT

There's no mention in 1 Thessalonians of the fullness of the Spirit or of the gifts which he grants. He appears as a quiet, unobtrusive Spirit to these Thessalonian Christians. He's active among them; without him nothing would have happened at all – no new birth, no Christian growth. It's possible that there were dramatic experiences similar to those in Corinth, but we hear nothing of them. It's equally possible that the Lord himself is teaching us that we don't have to look for ecstatic demonstrations in every situation to recognise that the Spirit is around. He is there, quietly at work, as well as sometimes being actively evidenced.

In 1946 I landed on an airstrip at Baroda in India to join a conversion course for flying Dakotas. That evening I was playing snooker in the Mess when someone invited me to a service in the camp chapel. It was Sunday and the last evening of some special meetings which had been arranged for the RAF station. As I sat listening to the speaker that night, nothing much registered until one sentence hit me hard. 'God can control your thoughts,' he said. I knew in an instant that, for a long time, God had had no important place in my thinking. There was deep conviction that God was speaking to me again directly through his Spirit. That night I had to ask God for cleansing, for restoration, for guidance concerning the way he wanted me to live in the future. His Holy Spirit that night made all that Jesus had done for me come again into focus, and I knew that God was speaking to me as his Spirit worked in my life. He took truth that I had known for many years – truth I had believed but so often had disobeyed – and made it real once more in an instant of compelling power.

THE HOLY SPIRIT MAKES THE TRUTH REAL

It's this amazing fact about the Holy Spirit's activity which surfaces right at the beginning of Paul's first letter to the Thessalonians. He comes as the Spirit who makes the truth real, and he brings conviction with it. Paul makes it clear that from the start of our Christian experience, the Holy Spirit is there working away at the centre of our lives. This is clearly seen in chapter 1, verses 4, 5:

> 'Brothers loved by God, we know that he has chosen you, because our gospel came to you not simply with words, but also with power, with the Holy Spirit and with deep conviction.'

There are two very significant words in these verses, and they are grouped on either side of the Holy Spirit. He was made known to the Thessalonians with *power* and with *deep conviction*. Those two realities vividly describe the Holy Spirit's activity. It was with this kind of power and conviction that the good news which Paul shared with them took shape in their lives.

The fact that Paul could present the good news with a power that rocked people to their roots, was not a demonstration of his own personal charisma – anything but, if 1 Corinthians 2:4 and 2 Corinthians 10:10 are an indicator. It was the direct fulfilment of Jesus' promise to his disciples recorded in Acts 1:8. The Lord Jesus at the moment of his return to heaven assured his followers:

> ' . . you will receive power when the Holy Spirit
> comes on you; and you will be my witnesses in
> Jerusalem, and in all Judea and Samaria, and to the
> ends of the earth.'

This revolutionising power was being released as Paul shared the good news about Jesus in Thessalonica. Consistently the Holy Spirit is seen as the person whom God uses to bring men, women and young people to the knowledge of Christ's salvation. This happened again and again as Paul went from city to city telling about Jesus.

This power was constantly evident, though it expressed itself in different ways. In Philippi, the city from which Paul had come to Thessalonica, there had been that terrifying earthquake while he and Silas were in prison. The walls were shattered, and an equally shattered jailor found himself kneeling before them, asking how he could be saved! He discovered that the Holy Spirit can take you, as it were, by the scruff of the neck, shatter your life around you, and bring you to an awareness of your need of salvation.

The same power of God's Spirit was there to save

Lydia – also in Philippi – but it came in a very different way. His powerful touch came quietly as she met with others down by the river. We read in Acts 16:14 that: 'The Lord opened her heart to respond to Paul's message.' In her case, there was a gentle work of God's Spirit, as he opened up her life like a flower.

The Holy Spirit comes with power; meeting people in their various areas of need, in a way which they can understand and respond to. John Wesley recalls how on May 24th, 1738, in the little meeting house in Aldersgate Street, London, he felt his heart strangely warmed as he listened to Martin Luther's introduction to Paul's letter to the Romans being read. That, too, was a work of God's Spirit, with his warming power, acting on John Wesley's life.

Luke, as he records the Thessalonians' experience in Acts 17:4, puts it like this: 'Some of the Jews were persuaded and joined Paul and Silas . . .' Does it sound pedestrian, almost casual? Not a bit of it! The Holy Spirit was there working deep in their minds and hearts. He *persuaded* them of the truth. There was power to release them from sin and from the domination of Satan. It's still happening – in a wide variety of ways. He works in different ways with our different temperaments and personalities. He makes his approach, fully aware of our background, our age-group, the situation in which we find ourselves. Don't stereotype or straitjacket the Holy Spirit! He comes with a power that meets our need.

• Think back over your own experience. How did you come to Christ? What was the evidence in your life of the Holy Spirit's activity?

As well as power, there's also conviction when the Holy

119

Spirit is at work, and this characterised God's work among the Thessalonian Christians. They were convicted deeply that the message Paul bought to them was true. They were convicted also that they were sinners, and that they needed Jesus the Christ to release them from sin. This was the point Paul made as he taught in the synagogue, 'explaining and proving that the Christ had to suffer and rise from the dead'. Conviction led to persuasion which rapidly and predictably led to persecution. Christ had faced it, so had Paul and Silas — now the Thessalonians. However, the Holy Spirit doesn't desert us when the pressure's on. Immediately, he makes his presence felt as Paul records in chapter 1, verse 6:

> 'You became imitators of us and of the Lord; in spite of severe suffering, you welcomed the message with the joy given by the Holy Spirit.'

THE HOLY SPIRIT GIVES JOY UNDER PRESSURE

It was tough. There were enemies, there was opposition, but the Holy Spirit was there, deep in their experience, giving them a joy that nothing else could explain.

Now, where do we fit in? Joy sounds great. And there's plenty of it around; in the fellowship, as we study God's word in our house groups and talk together over a church barbeque. There's also joy in helping each other, even when it includes a sense of pain.

● Think of the occasions, though, when joy tends to run out. What about outreach? Not necessarily holding forth on a street corner; there are our friends and people we see daily. We want to share the good news about Jesus, but how will they react? Joy? Suddenly, it's drained away like water down the plug-hole! Apprehension, a hollow feeling inside, fear – that begins to describe things.

● Here's something to pray about; and it won't end with praying. Remember the sequence of events when you heard about Jesus, and finally responded. It may not have been identical to the Thessalonians' experience, but there was power and conviction. And you were persuaded. Who was behind it all? God's Holy Spirit. He made the truth real, and he brought joy. Isn't it reasonable to pray that the same Holy Spirit who touched you and everyone else in the fellowship will also work in the minds and hearts of those around you who don't yet know him? Pray that he'll prepare homes and families, individuals, colleagues. The Spirit isn't locked up in New Testament characters like Lydia, the jailor and the Thessalonian church. He's alive and on the move in our local situations.

Fear had really got to June. The visiting team was due to call on homes around the church. She wanted to join in. But how? How to put things across? How to answer questions? How to handle hostility? Not much joy there.

Two of them went together. As they stood at the first door and knocked, June prepared to turn on her heels and run as the door was being opened. They introduced themselves, mentioned the church they were representing. Imagine their surprise and relief when the lady at the door responded, 'Well, isn't that interesting! I was only saying to my husband this morning, that no one ever comes from the churches around here and calls

121

on us. You're welcome! What have you got to tell me?' June made the thrilling discovery that the Holy Spirit had been there in advance, preparing the lady for her knock on the door. Of course, the response isn't always positive. There are hostile reactions, but we are called to pray that God will be at work, preparing those to whom we go. And the Holy Spirit, as June vividly discovered, gives real deep joy and happiness as the good news is shared.

We've seen how the Thessalonians experienced that joy in chapter 1, verse 6. Although we've thought a lot about opposition in these chapters, we've noted, too, the joy that we can experience as the Holy Spirit works in our lives and in the situations we face. We have good reason to expect it, for this joy is, of course, part of the Holy Spirit's fruit, the outworking of his presence in our lives.

Nehemiah once said, 'The joy of the Lord is your strength', and it is! Paul and the Thessalonians discovered it, even in suffering. There's nothing superficial here; it's a deep-down reality. Most of us enjoy security, and opposition isn't usually thrust on us. It's different for vast numbers of Christians overseas. As I looked into the lined faces of 700 Russian believers in one of Kiev's Baptist churches, I was left in no doubt about their joy which had strengthened them through years of opposition.

Suspicion, rejection and persecution have been the recurring experience of many in the Muslim world. It was in 1965 that war broke out between India and Pakistan. Living close to the border in the city of Lahore, Rahmat Masih came under pressure. He worked for the railway, and as a Christian involved in essential transport responsibilities for the government, he found himself under suspicion. The charge was colla-borating with the enemy. Quickly, Rahmat found him-self in jail, imprisoned in the old fort in Lahore.

The church prayed for him. On the Sunday morn-ing we came together early to intercede for Rahmat before the morning worship service. Time passed quickly as we prayed, pleading for his release. Our prayers ended, and we turned to join the service. But as we turned, there we saw him: Rahmat had joined the group, sitting behind us as we prayed! He had been released, and had come to the church, straight from jail – in time to hear the intercessions of those who loved him and cared about him. The joy we all experienced was overwhelming, his tears adding content to the inner thrill of knowing that in his release God had a powerful hand. There was joy given by the Holy Spirit that day.

It could have been anywhere in Eastern Europe, the Soviet Union, Romania, Bulgaria, Czechoslovakia, Poland, East Germany. For years it was a common experience for men and women to be harassed or arrested because they were Christians. In some countries the pressure is still on.

We may experience different pressures, different opposition as we seek to live for Jesus Christ in our office situations, and as we contact people around us. But whatever the response, favourable or tough, that same joy is available which comes from knowing that the Holy Spirit is at work, helping, strengthening, guid-ing, upholding. It's a joy that God gives, sometimes mingled with gratitude or relief or satisfaction – the joy of the Spirit.

This word 'joy' comes several times in Paul's letter. We find it first of all in chapter 1, verse 6. Then there's chapter 2, verses 19, 20, where Paul refers to the joy he will experience on meeting them all again when the Lord returns. And that joyous reunion will never end! Chapter 3, verse 9 highlights the joy they already bring him, for Timothy has just brought Paul the tremendous news that they are standing firm as Christians. Paul's overjoyed!

Look a little more closely, though, at the three-word verse in chapter 5, verse 16:

'Be joyful always.'

Quite a tall order, and it's only possible through the Holy Spirit. The plain fact is that we don't always feel joyful, and that could be said of Paul, too. He didn't have that bubbling effervescent joy which so many of us wish we could capture and live with permanently. Very honestly, he tells the Corinthians: 'I came to you in weakness and fear, and with much trembling' (1 Corinthians 2:3). That's not all. He goes on in his second letter:

> 'We do not want you to be uninformed, brothers, about the hardships we suffered in the province of Asia. We were under great pressure, far beyond our ability to endure, so that we despaired even of life. Indeed, in our hearts we felt the sentence of death. But this happened that we might not rely on ourselves but on God, who raises the dead.'
>
> *2 Corinthians 1:8, 9*

No superficial, surface joy there: 'great pressure . . . despair of life . . . sentence of death.' That's how they *felt*. No immediate way out – except to God. The last sentence in verse 9 is of fundamental importance. No matter what the problem, however intense the opposition, God is there – with us, right up to death and beyond. He 'raises the dead.' It's in this that Paul will find his security and joy. Verses 10 and 11 add to this conviction: 'He has delivered us from such a deadly peril, and he will deliver us. On him we have set our hope that he will continue to deliver us, as you help us by your prayers . . .' Deep down inside there's the joy of certainty and hope.

'Be joyful always.' Not easy, but a reality through the Holy Spirit God has given us. That had been Paul's discovery in Philippi. You can imagine him and Silas shackled inside the town prison, their backs sore and bleeding from the lashing they had received. Yet we read in Acts 16:25: 'About midnight Paul and Silas were praying and singing hymns to God, and the other prisoners were listening to them.' There was a deep, inner joy that only the Holy Spirit could give, and it enabled them to sing, even though they were suffering. So he writes from personal experience: 'Be joyful always.'

● It's quite easy to be joyful when everything is going well, or when we're in a worship group and others around us have joy written all over their faces. We're caught up in it, too. But joy is meant to extend to *every* experience of life. 'Always' places this joy at a different level and at a different quality. It's ours – the Holy Spirit's joy.

We have a friend, largely crippled with arthritis; always in pain, often excruciating pain. As we talk, her face is often alight with joy. There's laughter, too. We can never leave her feeling sad – though we have an inner ache which synchronises with her agony – her joy is infectious, and we praise God for the work of his Spirit in her life.

THE HOLY SPIRIT GIVES POWER FOR HOLY LIVING

As God works away at our lives he has many objectives. He aims through his Spirit to turn us into joyous people! That's good; the world needs to see real joy in action. The world also needs to see something else; holy people. And it's the Holy Spirit who gives us the power we need to live holy lives day by day. Paul reminds the Thessalonian Christians of this in chapter 4, verses 7, 8, where he writes:

> '. . . God did not call us to be impure but to live a holy life. Therefore, he who rejects this instruction does not reject man but God, who gives you his Holy Spirit.'

When we were thinking about holiness earlier, we recognised the tremendous pressure which our society exerts on us to be unholy – not least, to be sexually immoral. The Thessalonians knew the same pressures. Paul reminds them of God's call – his *demand* – to be holy. That's in verse 7. Difficult? Maybe. But God never demands the impossible. Verse 8 spells out the answer: 'God . . . gives you his Holy Spirit.' We can reject God's demand if we will – and many do – but the Holy Spirit's help is there. So, although living in today's world has it's problems, the Holy Spirit is adequate and able to meet us and to help us in every situation. He is given to make us holy, and because he is given to us, there's no need for us to give in to the pressures we experience.

When we were thinking about holiness we looked at 1 Corinthians 6:18, with its words: 'Flee from sexual immorality.' But Paul doesn't stop there. He goes on in the next two verses to explain why we're to flee:

> 'All other sins a man commits are outside his body, but he who sins sexually sins again his own body. Do you not know that your body is a temple of the Holy Spirit, who is in you, whom you have received from God? You are not your own: you were bought at a price. Therefore honour God with your body.'

It's encouraging as well as challenging to know that my body is the Holy Spirit's temple – his home. He lives in each of us and wants us to keep his home clean. He's only too ready to give us the help we need. If we want to be holy, it's wholly possible.

What a tremendous relief and joy it is to be released from the pressure of contemporary society to conform to its standards. For years the society in which we live has been called a permissive society. It's a lie. Our society is not permissive, it sets out to pressure us into unholiness, to make us conform to the standards of the vast majority around us. But the Holy Spirit comes to set us free, to give us power for holy living. That's a tremendous release, and we're called to grow in this freedom, giving over our bodies daily to be used as his temple.

THE HOLY SPIRIT IS TO BE OBEYED

It's tragically easy to listen to the Holy Spirit's voice, and then turn our backs on him, or conveniently 'forget' what he says. But the Holy Spirit is someone to be obeyed. In chapter 5, verse 19 Paul writes: 'Do not put out the Spirit's fire.' We've already noted the fact that it's possible for a Christian to reject the command of God to live a holy life. It's possible to be disobedient, and then to experience the disastrous results of refusing to go God's way. None of us is immune to this. No matter who we are, we're all subject to these pressures – from the most senior leader to the newest member of the congregation.

Some time ago I was in a town on the Welsh borders. After the morning service, during the coffee break, two little children were running around, while their father stood to one side – alone. When we got home I asked the pastor where the children's mother was, as I hadn't seen her with her husband. A tragic story unfolded as the pastor explained that the father of the two youngsters now had no wife. She had been going through problems, and the previous pastor had been counselling her. She had been greatly helped, but as the counselling proceeded, their relationship evolved into a friendship, which in turn deteriorated into a wrong relationship. Adultery followed. The pastor left, and the children's mother left with him.

The Holy Spirit is in us to be obeyed. The Spirit's fire is not to be put out. And no one is immune to temptation, in this or any other area of life.

It could be the love of money in a society which puts so much emphasis on possessions. Paul makes that clear to Timothy:

'People who want to get rich fall into temptation and a trap and into many foolish and harmful desires that plunge men into ruin and destruction. For the love of money is a root of all kinds of evil. Some

> people, eager for money, have wandered from the
> faith and pierced themselves with many griefs.'
>
> *1 Timothy 6:9, 10*

That's another route down which we can go, and put
out the Spirit's fire.

Our problem might not be money. It could be lying
or stealing, it could be any of the works of our sinful
nature which Paul refers to in Galatians 5:19–21. Or
we could find our weakness listed in Colossians 3:5–9
– impurity, lust, evil desires, greed, anger, rage, malice,
slander, filthy language. They all put out the Spirit's
fire. We find a similar list in Ephesians 4:31,32, where
Paul writes:

> 'Get rid of all bitterness, rage and anger, brawling
> and slander, along with every form of malice. Be
> kind and compassionate to one another, forgiving
> each other, just as in Christ God forgave you.'

It's in verse 30, from which these two verses flow,
that Paul puts his finger on the essential point, writing:
'. . . do not grieve the Holy Spirit of God, with whom
you were sealed for the day of redemption.'

It's tragically possible to reject God's command
and so to grieve the Holy Spirit of God, putting out his
fire. We know it from personal experience, and the
Devil concentrates his efforts to achieve it. But it's equally – gloriously – possible to obey the Spirit. That's
what we're re-made for! After referring to the Holy
Spirit's fruit in Galatians 5:22,23, Paul makes a strong
affirmation:

> 'Against such things there is no law. Those who
> belong to Christ Jesus have crucified the sinful

129

nature with its passions and desires. Since we live by the Spirit, let us keep in step with the Spirit.'

Keeping in step with the Spirit implies a daily walk with him, a walk characterised by obedience. While each day has its share of temptations, so also each day has the Holy Spirit's provision of power and strength to keep walking with him; not putting out his fire, but fanning it into a flame.

• If, however, we do fail and his fire is quenched, there is a way back. The fire bursts once more into flame as in our sorrow we confess, receive cleansing, discover the reality of the Spirit's restoration, get up and go on.

That's what growing in the Spirit is all about. We're people who are very conscious of our weaknesses, and our proneness to failure, but as we grow in the Spirit, we become increasingly conscious of his power to strengthen us, to help us as we walk in step with him, to please him, and to become like our Lord Jesus Christ.

8
GROW
THROUGH
PRAYER

We know it; prayer is for every situation – in joy, in sorrow; in the routine and the mundane; in the crisis experience. We're encouraged to come with our requests, and with our thanks as well. We have a heavenly Father who loves to give good gifts to his children. We know it, and too easily forget it. Especially when things are going well. Then he nudges us – perhaps because we have a problem – and he urges us to come . . .

Joanne and I were sitting on the floor of our little cabin on board the Anchor Line vessel 'Caledonia'. Our three boys bounced over the bunks as we typed out letter – a letter to God! Pakistan was just a few days away as we left Aden and turned eastward into the Arabian Sea. We were on our way back for the second time. God had given us so much. It was great – everything we needed – even a car. There it was safely down in Caledonia's hold. We'd watched them load it from Liverpool's dockside. It would be a tremendous help in and around Lahore, and we were running out of places to fit extra saddles and seats on our two bikes to cope with our growing family. Fantastic! God is good!

Then came the news. A letter from Colin Blair had been waiting for us in Aden, confirming a report that customs duty on cars had just been raised to 100%. What should we do? Cable our church? Our parents? It didn't seem right. God had given us the car, and a third of the value to cover customs. Surely, he hadn't made a mistake. He must have known. 'Well, he's provided all our needs so far,' we reasoned, 'and we've never asked for a penny. He'll send us all we need when we get to Karachi.' So, sitting on the cabin floor, we typed our letter to God, dated March 16th 1958 – our prayer to a God who hears! 'God, it's over to you.'

No sooner were we docked at Karachi than I was down at the purser's office to collect the incoming mail – mail that would contain all the money we needed! There were letters, too. One after another we opened them. Nothing, not a cheque, not a note fell out. Faith failed. We stood on deck, watching car after car being hoisted out of the hold, and lowered to the quayside. There was the Hillman Husky. It joined the others awaiting clearance. As we passed through customs there was nothing to pay, until the big question came.

'Sir,' asked the customs officer, 'is this everything? No unaccompanied baggage?'

'No. But there's just the matter of a car. Ours is out on the quayside.'

'Ah!' His eyes gleamed! 'How many doors does it have?' Why do customs officers ask such stupid questions?

'Three,' I replied. It didn't really matter if there were a dozen. So far as we were concerned it was already government property.

'Ah! Three doors. And where are they?' I nearly suggested they were in the roof, but wisdom prevailed. It's not wise to provoke customs officers.

'Well, there are two in the sides and one in the back.'

'Sir, you're a very lucky man.' And his gleaming eyes were matched by the widest of smiles. 'Do you know, sir, that customs duty has gone up on cars? Up to 100%. That is, on saloon cars. On estate cars and station waggons – anything having a rear-opening door – it's down to 30%! Sir, you are a very lucky man!'

Thank you, God. And we thought you had given up on us. Not a bit of it; he'd given us 3⅓% above our customs needs which was our petrol money to get us to Lahore and well beyond.

We still have that letter to remind us of a loving heavenly Father who does answer prayer, though frequently in ways we aren't expecting. He does know. He does care and he's not caught out by changing circumstances. And when our faith fails, he is still faithful.

So right there on Karachi docks we had a praise and thanksgiving session. And that's where prayer has to begin.

PRAYER STARTS WITH THANKSGIVING

In 1 Thessalonians Paul doesn't give a course on how to become a successful pray-er. But he does make some important points, and is himself a personal example. As we turn to Paul's letter we find that his prayers usually begin with thanksgiving. We have it in chapter 1, verse 2:

'We always thank God for all of you, mentioning you in our prayers.'

God certainly deserves our thanks, and he's the focus of Paul's gratitude. In all that has happened, Paul has seen his great and mighty God as the prime mover, and he gives him thanks for that. As we've seen in chapter 1, verses 4, 5, he's the God who initiates love, he's the God who chooses, he's the God who sends his powerful Spirit to convict, to convince and to save. Paul gives him thanks.

For his own part, Paul works hard. This surfaces in chapter 2, verse 9, where he refers to his toil and hardship, recalling how he worked night and day in order not to be a burden to anyone while he preached the gospel. But it wasn't *his* hard work which was ultimately effective. The effective power was *God's*. It was God who worked in the hearts and lives of those Thessalonian Christians. This was true, too, of the Corinthians. He writes:

'I planted the seed, Apollos watered it, but God made it grow. So neither he who plants nor he who waters is anything, but only God, who makes things grow.'
1 Corinthians 3:6, 7

Paul expands on this when he writes to the Philippians. He's confident that:

'. . . he who began a good work in you will carry it on to completion until the day of Christ Jesus.'
Philippians 1:6

So as Paul gets down to prayer he starts with thanksgiving, for God is the one who initiates his work, who continues it and who brings all his plans to a glorious conclusion. That's good reason for making sure that our prayers reflect our thankfulness.

It often helps to remind ourselves of reasons for thanksgiving. First of all we can concentrate on God himself – who he is and what he's done.

● Think of God's names and descriptions. We don't have to look far in Paul's letter and the rest of the New Testament to find words to fuel our thanks; he's Father, Holy Father, Father of compassion, God of all comfort, Righteous Father, he's merciful, he loves, he forgives, he strengthens, he's kind, the Father of Jesus, he guides and leads, he's Shepherd, King, powerful, understanding, Saviour, Lord, Redeemer. Can you think of others?
● Remember what he's done: he's sent his Son to save us and keep us day by day; he's given us his Holy Spirit to make us holy; remember details of his patience with you . . . let the list grow.
● What about the practical help he's given in the past week or month, in our family, at work? Note down the facts; they're all good reasons to be thankful. Sometimes we feel a bit down or depressed, and thanks don't come spontaneously. It's then that a list of reminders can get us started. Of course, there will be other times when we won't need any prodding or prompting, when praise and thanks will flow. But however we feel, God deserves our thanks.

PRAYER CONCERNS PEOPLE

It won't be long before people figure in our prayers. They, too, are an immediate cause for thanksgiving. Look again at Paul's letter. We read:

'We always thank God for *all of you*, mentioning *you* in our prayers.'   *1 Thessalonians 1:2*

And he repeats the emphasis in the next chapter:

'We also thank God continually because, when you received the word of God, which you heard for us, *you accepted it . . .* '   *1 Thessalonians 2:13*

He thanks God for their reaction to the good news, and the emphasis is on *all – everyone*. Everyone mattered to Paul: everyone needed prayer. This surfaces repeatedly in his various letters. To the Romans he writes:

'First, I thank my God through Jesus Christ for *all of you.*'   *Romans 1:8*

At that point he had never met them. But he included them all in his praying. In contrast, he knew the Corinthians very well, and right at the beginning of his letter he thanks God for his goodness to them; how they're 'enriched in every way' (1 Corinthians 1:4,5). To the Philippians, whom he also knew and loved, he writes, 'I thank my God every time I remember *you.*' (Philippians 1:3).

Constantly, their memory would come back to Paul, and he would remember them before God. As with the Romans, Paul, when he wrote to the Colossians, had never met them. Yet he's full of thanks to God because he's heard of their faith in Christ and of the love that they have for all the Christians (Colossians 1:3).

It's not just Christians worshipping together in churches, however, for whom Paul gives thanks. He writes to individuals – personal letters – and the same thanks bubble up. There's Timothy, whom he knows so intimately; and immediately there's thanksgiving.

> 'I thank God, whom I serve . . . as night and day *I constantly remember you in my prayers.*'
>
> *2 Timothy 1:3*

Then he goes on to list details for which he prays and also gives thanks.

Concern for people's needs

In chapter 6, I referred to Dr John Laird, whom I had found personally to be a tremendous example. This includes the place he gave to prayer. As General Secretary of Scripture Union he felt a deep responsibility for all his staff. He knew in amazing detail the lives of the men and women who worked for him, not only in the headquarters in London but those who were working in cities, towns and villages throughout the country. He listed each individual's situation, knew their work, understood their responsibilities. And he prayed. Day by day he would work through his lists, bringing them up to date, reorganising them, concentrating on the needs of those who were ultimately his responsibility. He became an example in prayer, just as Paul was to the Thessalonian Christians.

Similarly, our prayer records are meant to grow, develop and change. To the many items for thanksgiving we'll add details for requests and intercession.

- Think about people's daily circumstances, and how their lives are affected by them, where they live, how they travel, their work situations.
- Remember those who are unemployed, those we

137

know who are unwell, others who have a range of needs within their family situations, or as they live alone.

We all have needs

As we learn to pray, we discover that everyone has their own deep needs. So Paul prayed persistently and consistently for those with whom he was in contact. He was well aware of his own needs, too, and wasn't ashamed to ask people to pray for him. We get that brief request at the end of the first letter to the Thessalonians, where he writes: 'Brothers, pray for us.' In his second letter he expands on this, giving additional information:

> 'Finally, brothers, pray for us that the message of the
> Lord may spread rapidly and be honoured, just as
> it was with you. And pray that we may be delivered
> from wicked and evil men, for not everyone has faith.'
> *2 Thessalonians 3:1,2*

So Paul majors on detail; that of others and of his own situation.

• Take time to note down the detailed needs of those around you: personal needs, employment needs, health, family needs. It's quite a list, and it can be turned into prayer.

PRAYER IS AN ON-GOING RESPONSIBILITY

As we're caught up in the lives of those around us, we realise that prayer is an on-going responsibility and a privilege that we daren't give up. Paul emphasises this as he writes to the Thessalonians. One or two words highlight significantly the intensity with which he prays.

'We *always* thank God for all of you' (1 Thessalonians 1:2). And in the next verse he underlines this further when he writes, 'We *continually* remember before our God . . .' Chapter 3, verse 10 is even more specific: '*Night and day* we pray most earnestly that we may see you again and supply what is lacking in your faith.'

Keep at it

We're never to give up on our commitment to pray. Paul kept at it, though his days were full and time was precious. Take a look at his work programme. We see from chapter 2, verse 9 that he worked night and day in order not to be a burden on the Thessalonians. The trade which he had learned as a young man was tent-making, and he was able to earn his living in this way as he went around from place to place. Then there was the time he spent in direct evangelism, reaching out to people in the cities to which he went; talking on the busy streets. Added to that, he had a teaching programme for those who had come to know Jesus personally. And on top of everything, he was committed to prayer.

So it's significant that, with the kind of work load he carried, he could still say, '*Always* . . . *continually* we are praying for you.' This doesn't imply that he was shut up in a room for twenty-four hours a day, concentrating on a prayer ministry! He prayed while he was working, and while he was travelling. He prayed day and night, whenever he had the opportunity.

Quite often our prayer may be a request stemming from a deep longing in our hearts; it's there for months, or years and we bring it to God repeatedly. In other situations our prayers will rocket to God, sent on the spur of the moment of need. At other times we'll just be quiet in his presence. We discover we can come to him at any time, in any place.

A year or two ago we were skiing on the Kleine Scheidegg in Switzerland. It was the end of the week, and Sheila, who had learned to ski during those few days, was making the most of her last hours on the slopes. She stood on the crest of a descent, by the railway station, her skis pointing down the piste that leads to Wengen. It was a slope she had never tackled before. For a moment she hesitated. Then, waiting just behind her, I heard her prayer, 'Over to you, Lord!' And Sheila pushed off, her skis going straight, and she made it right to the bottom in good shape! God's there, at any time, in any place, and he listens to our thanksgiving, our requests, whatever it is we have to say.

We need a system

Off-the-cuff prayers are important. But it's equally important to have specific times and if possible a specific place where we can pray. That will be controlled by our work situation, our related lifestyle, and other commitments which we have to fulfil. But whatever our situation, we should work out a plan that's practical and one we can keep to. It may not be easy. Keeping regular prayer times rarely are, and Satan's against the idea, too.

● For some, it's easier to pray in the morning. Others are better able to spend a time with God before they go to bed. But that time of quietness in God's presence, when we can read and pray, is of immense importance.
● It's helpful if we can find a prayer partner. When Billy Graham last came to England, the Evangelical Alliance stressed the importance of Prayer Triplets, and

they produced booklets, as we've already noted, designed to help three people coming together to praise and pray for specific issues: for people, for situations, for personal needs. A whole range of items could be listed. To pray regularly with a prayer partner is a tremendous help, and it's a stimulus to keep us going.

• Of course, there are prayer sessions in our local church, or in a house-group or Christian Union. These can be valuable times when together we bring our thanks and requests to God.

• There can be family prayers too. When our children were all at home it was only possible, sometimes, to get together on Saturdays or Sundays for family prayers. At other times we managed to fit in prayer after our evening meal. Nowadays, Joanne and I are able to spend some time together after breakfast in the morning.

• It's important to keep our prayer information up to date. A notebook or loose-leafed folder can be used for this purpose. As Paul received more information, he added it to his prayer list. If you glance at 1 Thessalonians 1:3, you find that he thanks God as he remembers three things about the Thessalonians; their faith, their love, then their hope in the Lord Jesus. As more information came to him, through Timothy and possibly through other sources, he was able to add it to what he already knew. So we find that when he writes the second letter, he recalls in chapter 1, verse 3 that he's thanking God because their faith is growing more and more, he's thankful, too, because their love for each other is increasing. So we see that the information Paul has received has been built into his praying.

• It's important to plan our own programme within the limits of the time available, and to combine it with reading God's word. As we read, our thanksgiving is stimulated, our trust and expectation, too, are heightened, and our praying becomes increasingly meaningful.

PRAYER MUST BE SPECIFIC

As we keep our records up to date we'll be reminded again and again of how specific our praying needs to be. It's not just a matter of saying, 'God bless Mum and Dad,' or, 'Please bless Jo and Andrew,' and leaving it there. This comes through very strongly in Paul's Thessalonian letter. Look at the key passages again. Paul spells out an amazing range of details.

We've already seen how he prays in 1 Thessalonians 1: 3, and builds on it with more details in 2 Thessalonians chapter 1: 3 – a letter he wrote a few months later. As we work through his first letter, however, we find how specific he is. In chapter 3, verses 10–13 there's a series of prayer requests:

• that they might meet again to build up their faith (v 10);
• that God will take care of travel arrangements (v 11);
• that their love will increase for each other and for everyone else – the outsiders and persecutors (v 12);
• that God will strengthen them to be blameless and holy (v 13).

On into chapter 5, verse 23 we find more detailed requests:

• that God will sanctify them through and through – Paul doesn't pray for half-measures!
• that God will keep them totally blameless in spirit, soul and body – mentally, spiritually and physically.

We discover some repetition in Paul's prayers – about blamelessness, holiness and love. God doesn't mind us repeating ourselves. Notice, too, that Paul makes big requests. We've got a big God.

The usefulness of a notebook was proved when I was visiting the city of Multan in Pakistan a few years ago. Prayer was the subject in our evening session. After the meeting, seven converted Muslims came up to me. I had been emphasising the advantages of keeping a record of prayer needs, so that they could be remembered regularly before God. Each of those seven men came with a request: 'Please get out your book and enter my name.' Along with some of their names were details for prayer and thanksgiving.

Two years later I was back in the same city, and two of those men came along to another teaching session. They had new details to share. Anwar and Bashir had been under pressure. Alongside the local mosque Anwar had a small apartment where he and his friends frequently got together to worship the Lord. News leaked through to the mosque, and opposition escalated. An unsuccessful attempt was made on Anwar and Bashir's lives; the apartment was ransacked and destroyed. Finally, charges were registered against them with the police. Then at the height of the opposition the treasurer of the mosque, a Muslim, had gone to the police testifying to Anwar and Bashir's good character and uprightness. Finally, he secured their release on bail.

Recounting the details of these events, they asked for specific prayer. There were their own needs – for safety, power to witness, vindication in court – but at the head of their list was a special prayer request, more important to them than anything else. It was for the

Muslim treasurer of that mosque; thanking God for his kindness, his trustworthiness, and also with a special plea that he, too, might come to know the Lord Jesus Christ.

Their initial prayer request had gone straight into the notebook; their names a constant reminder of their needs. Now there were further details: matters for praise and thanksgiving, urgent requests for intercession. So a prayer diary comes alive, a constant reminder and a challenge and encouragement to keep praying.

People often come, as those two men came, with specific requests for prayer. As we noted in chapter 4, where we were thinking about commitment, it's all too easy to say, 'Yes, I'll pray for you.' But five minutes or five hours later we've forgotten all about it. It's not because we have no interest in praying; more often it's the pressure of events which just crowds things out of our minds. When they're written down they won't be forgotten so easily.

LOOK FOR ANSWERS

Along with making and keeping a record of requests, we can keep a record of answers, too. Look out for the ways in which God answers our prayers, because when we pray specifically, God answers specifically. We've seen in 1 Thessalonians 1: 2, 3 and in 2 Thessalonians 1: 3 how God answered those early prayers of the apostle. He rejoices in his second letter that their 'faith is growing more and more'.

In 1 Thessalonians 3: 12 he prays:

'. . . the Lord make your love increase and overflow for each other and for everyone else . . .'

And when he writes his second letter we find him giving thanks in chapter 1, verse 3:

'because . . . the love every one of you has for each other is increasing.'

Paul had prayed specifically, and God had answered specifically.

God has his own ways of answering which don't always fall into line with what we're expecting him to do. There was one occasion some years ago when a group with Oak Hall Expeditions was returning from Bavaria. Torrential rain had saturated everything and everyone during the final days of camp: young people, parents and children, tents, sleeping bags, equipment – nothing had escaped. When at last everything was finally packed away, and all were aboard, the bus set off for home. And still the rain bucketed down.

They were approaching Munich when it happened: the oil light on the dashboard shone red. Out in the drenching rain Ian Mayo checked the engine and his worst fears were realised – a fractured oil line. They were marooned for the night, for it was Saturday afternoon, garages were closed and no help was available. Ian asked the group to pray; but for what? No one was sure. But there was no doubt that fifty very wet young people, parents and children needed help urgently. They knew God could help, though one of the non-Christians on board was heard to say, 'If this is the way God looks after you all, I can do without him!'

Immediately opposite the bus, just where it had

lurched to a halt, a house was visible through the rain. Ian went to the door and knocked. Perhaps they might know of a barn where the group could shelter for the night.

A woman answered the knock, and Ian began to explain: 'Excuse me, but we have a problem. We've just broken down and I have fifty, very wet people on board. We've been camping and everything we have is soaked.' She looked totally stunned.

'We're a Christian home,' she explained, 'where orphans – boys and girls – come for their holidays. I've been expecting fifty of them to come this afternoon, but I've just put the phone down, having been told that they can't arrive until tomorrow morning. You're welcome! Come right in. I've got fifty beds all made up. They're ready for you.'

God answers prayer! They had prayed, not knowing how he could help, but firmly believing that he could and would. His answer was beyond their wildest expectations. And the sceptic was converted shortly afterwards!

God answers specific prayer in specific ways. And, he encourages us to keep on asking, because he delights to answer. As we see his specific answers we're encouraged to trust him increasingly with the needs of our lives. We grow in thankfulness, we grow in expectation, we grow in trust, we grow through prayer.

9

GROW IN EXPECTANCY

In times of stress, danger or persecution Christians have often turned their minds to the second coming. When will Christ return? Just outside Hanover, after the end of World War II, a camp was established for displaced persons; refugees from various parts of Europe. Hemmed in by endless coils of barbed wire, men and women, boys and girls waited anxiously. Many suffered from malnutrition and tuberculosis. All of them longed for a home and wondered if it would ever be provided. They seemed to be without hope, and many died daily. But that wasn't the total picture: there, gathered together close to the barbed wire, was a group of Christians, who lifted their hands to God daily, crying out, 'Come, Lord Jesus!' That was their hope. For them nothing else seemed to represent a remedy or a solution.

It's been the same in subsequent years, as men and women have endured the ravages of communism; it's been the same, too, for God's people, suffering under hostile, alien religions; many giving their lives as martyrs; all looking to that final act of salvation, when the Lord Jesus will appear from heaven.

On the other hand, prosperity, comfort, ease and tolerance have tended to diminish interest in the return of Jesus Christ.

However, during the New Testament period, and for many long years afterwards, Christian churches were under assault. And the Christians in Thessalonica were among the first to receive and experience the viciousness of hostility. As Paul writes to them – in both of his letters – Christ's return is a dominant theme.

IT'S FOR SURE!

Jesus Christ will come again – it's absolutely certain. That's the persistent message, but Paul gives no dates or times. His first letter to the Thessalonians highlights important features of Christ's return, and the second letter explains how certain events will develop.

Since Paul's departure from Thessalonica, a problem had arisen: either some of the Christians had died, or they were worried in case some should die before Christ returned. In that event, what would happen to them? Paul's immediate response is set out in chapter 4, verse 13, where he writes:

> 'Brothers, we do not want you to be ignorant about those who fall asleep, or to grieve like the rest of men, who have no hope.'

In answering, Paul highlights a contrast. Non-Christians he says have no hope, but for Christians the hope is certain. No matter what the situation, they could rejoice, for this brief word 'hope' spelt out certainty. Here there's a world of difference between English and Greek usage. Looking at the sky, we might well say, 'I hope it will stay fine.' But the very form of the sentence implies a doubt: 'I'm afraid it might rain.' However, there was no doubt for the Greeks: 'hope' for them implied fulfilment – certainty. Paul emphasised this at the very start of his letter. In chapter 1, verse 3 he referred to their work produced by faith, their labour prompted by love, and their 'endurance inspired by hope in our Lord Jesus Christ.'

These Christians were able to endure because their hope pointed with certainty to Christ's coming. In their minds, there was no doubt about it. That's the great hope which runs unerringly throughout the whole of the New Testament, and again and again down the centuries it has inspired Christian men and women in every adverse situation.

A HOPE TO SHARE

Not only were the Thessalonians convinced of it, they *shared* their conviction. Everyone they met got this message, and you'll recall how they reached out into the whole of Greece and beyond. Paul refers to that in chapter 1, verses 9, 10, recalling the reaction of those who heard the message which the Thessalonians brought:

> 'They tell how you turned to God from idols to serve
> the living and true God, and to wait for his Son
> from heaven, whom he raised from the dead – Jesus,
> who rescues us from the coming wrath.'

Three elements stand out, and this was the clear proclamation of the Thessalonians wherever they went: the

149

living Lord Jesus Christ will come back; he will rescue believers, but there will be wrath for others.

These facts are tremendously important, and Paul expands on them further as he writes his letter. In chapter 4, verse 17, speaking of believing Christians, he says:

'We who are still alive and are left will be caught up with them in the clouds to meet the Lord in the air. And so we will be with the Lord for ever.'

That's the great rescue plan for men and women who trust Jesus as their Saviour. But the wrath that is reserved for others is unfolded as Paul continues in chapter 5, verses 2, 3:

'You know very well that the day of the Lord will come like a thief in the night. While people are saying, "Peace and safety", destruction will come on them suddenly, as labour pains on a pregnant woman, and they will not escape.'

Paul himself and the Thessalonian Christians obviously found in this a powerful incentive for evangelism as they reached out to those around them. So it has remained ever since. If we really believe that God's word is true, then the inevitable challenge has to be faced.

Hudson Taylor, sensing God's call to China in 1850, wrote, 'Think of it – three hundred and sixty million souls, without God or without hope in the world! Think of more than twelve million of our fellow-creatures dying every year without any of the consolations of the gospel.' It was as if those millions were advancing over a precipice and falling to destruction below. But it wasn't only China that tore at Hudson

Taylor's heart. He ached for his own home town of Barnsley which John Wesley had visited on June 30th, 1786. 'I turned aside to Barnsley,' he wrote, 'formerly famous for all manner of wickedness. They were then ready to tear any Methodist preacher in pieces. Now not a dog wagged its tongue. I preached near the Market Place to a very large congregation, and I believe the truth sank into many hearts. They seemed to drink in every word.'

The fact that men and women were lost, that destruction was an impending reality, gripped both John Wesley and Hudson Taylor. They longed for all to be ready to face Jesus Christ at his coming or at death. Their longing created a vibrant Methodism, founded the China Inland Mission, and a living church in China. The same message and urgency has come through to the twentieth century. The motivation is still the same, for still there are millions marching unerringly toward destruction.

Paul, however, wrote, not so much with national or international evangelists in mind, but to very ordinary Thessalonian Christians – people who got up and went throughout the whole of Greece, sharing the good news of Jesus, God's Son, who is coming back from heaven to rescue us from the coming wrath (1: 10). So we have to ask ourselves what we are doing in our own area in the light of the same facts. The message is the same, God's power is the same, a great turning to Christ is the objective, but time is limited.

A GREAT REUNION

Jesus will come; it's certain. Some will be saved, others lost. But, for those who belong to Christ, it will be a great reunion. Look at the verses in 1 Thessalonians 4: 14–18:

> We believe that Jesus died and rose again and so we believe that God will bring with Jesus those have fallen asleep in him. According to the Lord's own word, we tell you that we who are still alive, who are left till the coming of the Lord, will certainly not precede those who have fallen asleep. For the Lord himself will come down from heaven, with a loud command, with the voice of the archangel and with the trumpet call of God, and the dead in Christ will rise first. After that, we who are still alive and are left will be caught up with them in the clouds to meet the Lord in the air. And so we will be with the Lord for ever. Therefore encourage each other with these words.'

Six important facts emerge from these verses:

• Believers who have died or 'fallen asleep in him' will come back with the Lord Jesus. It's apparent from Philippians 1: 23 and 2 Corinthians 5: 8 that our spirits go to be with Christ at death. However, when we return with him, we will receive new resurrection bodies. This is made clear in verse 16 when we read that 'the dead in Christ will rise first.'

• This won't be a hidden or obscure event; verse 16 is crystal clear – the 'loud command', the 'voice of the archangel' and the 'trumpet call of God' will be the greatest public announcement the world has ever heard! John, writing the book of the Revelation, describes it as he quotes from the Old Testament, 'Look, he is coming with the clouds, and every eye will see him, even those who pierced him' (Revelation 1: 7).

● All who belong to him will 'meet the Lord in the air.' And if that sounds fantastic, so it is!

● The fourth important fact immediately emerges: we shall 'be with the Lord for ever.'

● And all these facts are for our encouragement and joy – 'Therefore encourage each other with these words.' The Thessalonians were having a tough time. Opposition and harassment can be wearing and demoralising. But that wasn't the end of the road: Christ was coming back for a tremendous reunion. That was encouragement enough to press on and to live for Christ.

Our encouragement and joy are no less. The thought of actually seeing Jesus and being with him for ever takes my breath away! There will also be the tremendous joy of being united with other Christians from around the world, the greatest international gathering that the world has ever experienced. There will be the joy, too, of seeing those who brought you to know the Lord Jesus, and meeting again those whom you had the privilege of introducing to him. Paul is full of joy as he looks forward to being with the Thessalonian Christians in that ultimate reunion:

> 'For what is our hope, our joy, or the crown in which we will glory in the presence of our Lord Jesus Christ when he comes? Is it not you? Indeed, you are our glory and joy.'   *1 Thessalonians 2: 19, 20*

The Lord has a tremendous reunion in store for us.

• The sixth emphasis is implied rather that stated in these verses. It's this: we'll be made completely perfect when we meet him. There's no other way that we could spend eternity with the Lord Jesus. Paul was anxious that they should be adequately prepared for that tremendous event, so he prays in chapter 3, verse 13:

> 'May he strengthen your hearts so that you will be blameless and holy in the presence of our God and Father when our Lord Jesus comes with all his holy ones.'

There's certainly no doubt that we will be changed to be like Jesus Christ. Paul makes this abundantly clear when he writes to the Corinthians in 1 Corinthians 15, but nevertheless they are to work at being blameless and holy right now, as they live for Jesus Christ. John underlines this when he writes his first letter, chapter 3, verses 2, 3:

> 'Dear friends, now we are children of God, and what we will be has not yet been made known. But we know that when he appears, we shall be like him, for we shall see him as he is. Everyone who has this hope in him purifies himself, just as he is pure.'

That gives us something to work on as we look towards this tremendous reunion.

But there are two important questions which we have to ask ourselves: are we ready for Christ's coming? Is our expectation, our anticipation, our enthusiasm for it growing? It may be necessary to deal with sin that tarnishes and spoils our lives; to repent; to get right with friends or enemies. Let nothing spoil or dampen this certain hope, as we look forward to the coming of the Lord Jesus Christ. It's this need which Paul goes on immediately to deal with. We're to be ready for Christ's coming. He spells out the details in chapter 5, verses 1–11.

UNEXPECTED BY MILLIONS

In the first three verses of chapter 5 he reminds us that the coming of Jesus will be unexpected by the world's millions. See what he writes:

> 'Now, brothers, about times and dates we do not need to write to you, for you know very well that the day of the Lord will come like a thief in the night. While people are saying, "Peace and safety", destruction will come on them suddenly, as labour pains on a pregnant woman, and they will not escape.'

As that day approaches, it's probable that the United Nations and the European Community will still be organising peace conferences, still be pronouncing peace formulas. Yet all the time anarchy will increasingly stamp its mark on the world around us as social structures crumble, law and order collapses, and ethnic, political and religious groupings fight. It's in that deepening darkness that Christ will come.

In his second letter, Paul goes on to elaborate:

> 'Don't let anyone deceive you in any way, for that day will not come until the rebellion occurs and the man of lawlessness is revealed, the man doomed to destruction. He opposes and exalts himself over everything that is called God or is worshipped, and

> even sets himself up in God's temple, proclaiming
> himself to be God.' *2 Thessalonians 2: 3, 4*

It's at that moment of disaster when 'the lawless one'
– the anti-christ – seems all-powerful, when evil appears
overwhelming, that the Lord Jesus Christ will come in
all his power and glory. Paul describes it in 2 Thessalonians 2:8:

> '. . . the lawless one will be revealed, whom the Lord
> Jesus will overthrow with the breath of his mouth
> and destroy by the splendour of his coming.'

Tragically, many who have lined themselves up with
evil will be lost. As Paul indicates: 'destruction will
come on them suddenly'. It's another incentive to us to
reach out with the good news of forgiveness while we
have the opportunity.

LIVE FOR JESUS

Though the tragedy will be immense – beyond anything
we could describe – it need not take us by surprise.
We've been forewarned. The apostle spells it out in
chapter 5, verses 4, 5:

> 'But you, brothers, are not in darkness so that this
> day should surprise you like a thief. You are all
> sons of the light and sons of the day. We do not
> belong to the night or to the darkness.'

Not in darkness; brought into light. We've got our eyes
open. That's what Paul assures us. So we're to live with
this constant expectation: Jesus Christ is coming back!

So while we wait, what sort of lifestyle does Jesus look for? The guidelines come through clearly in 1 Thessalonians 5: 1–11 – the section we're concentrating on. Look now at verses 6–11:

> 'So then, let us not be like others, who are asleep, but let us be alert and self-controlled. For those who sleep, sleep at night, and those who get drunk, get drunk at night. But since we belong to the day, let us be self-controlled, putting on faith and love as a breastplate, and the hope of salvation as a helmet. For God did not appoint us to suffer wrath but to receive salvation through our Lord Jesus Christ. He died for us so that, whether we are awake or asleep, we may live together with him. Therefore encourage one another and build each other up, just as in fact you are doing.'

There are five key words to get hold of here. And they form valuable guidelines for living as we prepare for Jesus' return.

● *Be alert* – wide awake. It's a tip-toe stance of expectancy. Altogether the Greek word occurs twenty-three times in the New Testament, but only twice does the New International Version render it 'Be alert'. The other occasion is in Peter's warning: '. . . be alert. Your enemy the devil prowls around . . .' (1 Peter 5: 8). Keep your eyes open for him. He's dangerous. Twice it's translated 'Be on your guard', but in every other case the word is 'Watch . . . !' and it usually refers to Jesus' second coming. Jesus himself used it when he told the parable of the ten virgins (Matthew 25: 1–13), and about the man who had his house broken into (Matthew 24: 42–44) – both illustrating Christ's return.

These two parables mirror a common attitude. The second coming doesn't happen, and Christians get sleepy. After all, life's pretty comfortable. Relax. It won't happen yet. There are lots of things to concentrate on – career, keeping the mortgage going, family joys, problems and responsibilities, plus a hundred and one other valid and important issues. Certainly give each its proper place, but Jesus still insists: 'Watch! Keep alert! I'm coming back. Be ready for me.'

How do we work it out? Well, the remaining four words help us to set priorities.

● *Be self-controlled.* Make sure that your choices are worthwhile. In Verse 7 Paul is talking about 'sleepy' people and those who 'get drunk'; these are night-time activities, but we're 'day people' – 'sons of the light and sons of the day' (v 5).

It was late afternoon when I saw him outside Victoria station in London. I suppose he was in his early forties – ragged, torn clothes, tangled hair, unkempt beard streaked with grey. He staggered on unsteady feet, swore at the rush-hour crowds, lurched as he lifted his bottle for another swig. Self-control was gone. Its loss can be expressed in various ways, but for Paul and us, too, drunkenness highlights and illustrates the contrast between self-control and chaos.

Through his Spirit, Jesus gives us decision-making power to work out our priorities; recognising what Christ wants us to do with our lives as we look forward to his coming. This means, saying 'no' to selfishness, greed, or whatever temptation Satan may throw at us, and 'yes' to all that will enable us to look Jesus in the face when we see him.

The final three words give us all the positive incentives for decision-making and action that we need – faith, love and hope.

● *Faith* sets us on course. Faith initially saves, keeps us going and believes with equal assurance that Jesus is coming back. Faith also implies faithfulness, which helps us to be true to him. So it's an important part of self-control.

● *Love* will be an unfailing friend and guide as we prepare ourselves for Jesus' return. We'll do those things we know will please him. We'll be alert and on the look-out for signs of his coming. We want to meet him face to face, because we love him. Jesus said: 'If you love me, you will obey what I command' (John 14: 15). Is there a stronger motive for self-control?

● *Hope* is sure. It doesn't give up. No matter how long it takes, how tough life gets, hope grows if it's genuine. It was the hope – the certainty – of Jesus' return that kept the Thessalonians going. Our hope of salvation will be complete when Jesus comes back (5:8). It's hope which motivates a pastor from Canton. Three years ago his church was growing and, so it seemed, was freed to live for Christ. Then came Tiananmen Square and the consequent backlash. Today the church is bulldozed. The pastor is in prison – possibly with a death sentence. But there is no weakening of hope. He knows he's going to meet Jesus, either when he returns, or before.

So for that pastor and for ourselves, faith, love and hope form an indispensable and adequate armour; a breastplate and helmet, protecting our hearts and minds, as we commit ourselves to living for Jesus until he comes.

ENCOURAGEMENT

There must be times when that Canton pastor falters. He may be in isolation; he knows that an inflexible and hostile regime is lined up against him, and Satan's on the offensive. The Thessalonians knew all about hostility, and we ourselves face it in various ways. But whatever our situation we need to remember, 'God did not appoint us to suffer wrath but to receive salvation through out Lord Jesus Christ' (v 9). God does not desert us. He's on our side. Close to a pastor in prison. Alongside us wherever we are, to strengthen and help us whatever our need. Salvation will be complete when he comes.

Verse 10 covers all eventualities: the Lord Jesus Christ 'died for us so that, whether we are awake or asleep, we may live together with him.' Living together with Jesus is the ultimate to which we look forward, and it will become a glorious and total reality when he returns.

With this in mind Paul says, '. . . encourage one another and build each other up . . .' (v 11). Do just that – in your local fellowship and among your friends. Make the great news a talking point!

Of course, there's an important question which we have to answer: What does the second coming actually mean to us? Is it irrelevant? Is life too comfortable? Is it in some awesome way unattractive or fearsome? As we look into our lives, do we discover that we're not ready for it? Or, on the other hand, is our expectation growing? Can we say with enthusiasm, 'He really could be coming soon! I want to be ready for him'? It's in that expectancy that God wants us to grow.